# Managing By VALUES®

## KEN BLANCHARD
## MICHAEL O'CONNOR

### WITH
### JIM BALLARD

BERRETT-KOEHLER PUBLISHERS, INC.
San Francisco

**Berrett-Koehler Publishers, Inc.**
235 Montgomery Street, Suite 650
San Francisco, CA 94104-2916
Tel: (415) 288-0260  Fax: (415) 362-2512  www.bkconnection.com

**Ordering Information**

*Quantity sales.* Special discounts are available on quantity purchases by corporations, associations, and others. For details, contact the "Special Sales Department" at the Berrett-Koehler address above.

*Individual sales.* Berrett-Koehler publications are available through most bookstores. They can also be ordered direct from Berrett-Koehler: Tel: (800) 929-2929; Fax: (802) 864-7626; www.bkconnection.com

*Orders for college textbook/course adoption use.* Please contact Berrett-Koehler: Tel: (800) 929-2929; Fax: (802) 864-7626.

*Orders by U.S. trade bookstores and wholesalers.* Please contact Ingram Publisher Services, Tel: (800) 509-4887; Fax: (800) 838-1149; E-mail: customer.service@ ingrampublisherservices.com; or visit www.ingrampublisherservices.com/Ordering for details about electronic ordering.

Berrett-Koehler and the BK logo are registered trademarks of Berrett-Koehler Publishers, Inc.

Printed in the United States of America

Berrett-Koehler books are printed on long-lasting acid-free paper. When it is available, we choose paper that has been manufactured by environmentally responsible processes. These may include using trees grown in sustainable forests, incorporating recycled paper, minimizing chlorine in bleaching, or recycling the energy produced at the paper mill.

**Library of Congress Cataloging-in-Publication Data**
Blanchard, Kenneth H.
    Managing by values / Kenneth Blanchard. Michael O'Connor with Jim Ballard.
       p. cm.
    ISBN: 978-1-57675-007-0
    ISBN: 978-1-57675-274-6 (pbk.)
       1. Quality of work life—United States. 2. Corporate culture—United States. 3. Organizational change—United States.
    I. O'Connor, Michael J., 1944–  . II. Ballard, Jim. III. Title.
    HD6957.068549   1997
    658.4—dc21                 96-45613   CIP

First Hardcover Edition 1997
First Paperback Edition 2003
14  13  12  11  10          10  9  8  7  6  5  4  3

Copyediting: Mary Lou Sumberg. Proofreading: PeopleSpeak. Interior design and production: Joel Friedlander Publishing Services. Cover: Richard Adelson

# Contents

# Introduction

IN 1986, I PARTICIPATED in a convention where John Naisbitt gave a speech on his book *Reinventing the Corporation*, coauthored with his wife, Patricia Aburdeene. Toward the end of his speech, John shared his dream that "someday there will be a list of 'Fortunate 500' companies." I was immediately intrigued by this unusual, yet obviously intentional, play on words.

John went on to explain that while we all know that a Fortune 500 company is defined by its size and volume, a *Fortunate 500* company would be defined by the quality of service available to its customers and the quality of life accessible to its employees.

After his speech, I shared with John my fascination and excitement about the Fortunate 500 concept and asked him if he had done any real thinking about what qualified an organization as a Fortunate 500 company. He said he hadn't.

I suggested we get together to try to determine what defines a Fortunate 500 company and to see if we could find a way to identify companies or organizations that were on their way to becoming Fortunate 500 companies. John was intrigued by the idea, but at the time he and Patricia were working on their next book, *Megatrends 2000*, so he encouraged me to go ahead and pursue the Fortunate 500 concept on my own.

My first move was to speak with Mary Falvey Fuller, a fellow Cornellian. Mary had worked with McKinsey and Company, Inc., an international management consulting firm; she had also managed the operational side of organizations. As Mary and I reviewed many of the studies that had been done on "excellence," we found that whenever people talked about it, they focused on results—the key success indicators that suggested a company was a leader.

These indicators included the usual things like volume, profit, return on investment or assets, and the like. Typically, once the list of excellent companies was established based on their results, consultants and researchers next focused on the companies' management practices to identify what gave these organizations the kinds of results they were getting.

The more we investigated this concept of "excellence," the more we questioned its definition. We questioned it because we noticed how people's motivations and expectations were changing with respect to their work and how virtually every company was facing increasing complexity, competitive challenge, and rate of change. As we saw it, the practices that had produced the best results from the sixties through the eighties would not be effective in the nineties and beyond. Today's economy called for a new and broader approach. So we began to focus instead on what we believed to be the foundation of an effective organization—namely, its *mission* and its *values*.

Perhaps more than at any previous time, an organization today must know what it stands for and on what principles it will operate. No longer is values-based organizational behavior an interesting philosophical choice—it is a requisite for survival.

The particular mix of dilemmas in which competitive companies do business nowadays requires that they build success upon effectiveness. Once an organization has a clear picture of its mission and values, it has a strong basis for evaluating its management practices and bringing them into alignment with the articulated mission and values.

I got so excited about this Fortunate 500 concept that Norman Vincent Peale and I mentioned it in our book, *The Power of Ethical Management*. Erv Kamm, then president and chief operating officer at Norstan, a telecommunications company headquartered in Minneapolis, read about it in the copy of the book that Sid Cohen, chairman of that same company, had given him. They both became interested in how Norstan might become a Fortunate 500 organization, and Erv wrote us a letter to that effect. Mary Falvey

Fuller and I then visited with Erv, Paul Baszucki, and Richard Cohen at Norstan. The first Fortunate 500 project was begun.

It didn't take long for us to realize that the concept was a lot easier to describe than to effectively install. As a result, it became obvious we would need an expert on values-based interventions. That's where Michael O'Connor came into the picture.

While I was working on making the behavioral sciences come alive for people at work and at home, Michael had been methodically studying the practical application of insights about values. When I contacted him in 1990, he had already discovered the untapped power of values as an integrating force in the lives of highly effective individuals, work groups/teams, and organizations and was busy implementing this know-how with clients and other consultants.

I invited Michael to join Mary and me in helping organizations put our Fortunate 500 business philosophy into practice through his own process of *Managing By Values* (MBV). He accepted, and Norstan became our first joint Fortunate 500 project for the MBV process.

Michael had already begun an extensive intervention with the Holt Companies, a major Caterpillar distributor and gas compressor manufacturer headquartered in Texas. Peter Holt, chief executive officer of the Holt Companies, had been searching for some way to manage his company more effectively, leave a legacy that would survive beyond his leadership, and at the same time establish further congruency in his personal life. The Holt Companies soon became our second Fortunate 500 project.

We divided the duties. Michael focused on helping organizations articulate their corporate values and executives identify their personal values. He also devised systems for resolving misalignments between individual, work group, and corporate values. Mary zeroed in on identifying the strategic decisions and management practices where the fusion of values and an orientation toward results would be most powerful. I acted as spokesperson and cheerleader for the MBV process and for the top managers of our project companies.

Together, we worked with Norstan and Holt to address specific decisions and modify key practices to bring their walk in line with their talk. After about three years, Mary shifted her focus to coupling corporate strategy with management of change and organizational learning, while Michael and I teamed with my Blanchard Training and Development (BTD) colleagues, Fred Finch and Drea Zigarmi, to continue our work with Managing By Values.

In 1992, the Fortunate Companies Foundation was created as a nonprofit corporation for the purpose of promoting and perpetuating this management process in organizations. In a joint venture with BTD, the foundation is currently working with aspiring Fortunate 500 project companies on their Managing By Values journey. At the time of this writing, Michael serves as director of consulting services for the foundation's Center for Managing By Values.

As chairman of Blanchard Training and Development, I am the number one spokesperson and cheerleader for the Managing By Values process, while several of my BTD associates are working with Michael and other foundation consultants on its implementation.

I am an MBV believer because I have witnessed the significant payoff experienced by organizations undergoing the process. These organizations have developed clear mission statements and operating values and have communicated these values throughout their companies; their journeys have been all about managing by those values. The kinds of continuing success stories in the areas of performance, satisfaction, and return on investment are documented in this book. While it is written as a fictional account, the story is based on actual reports by the implementers, customers, and owners at Norstan, Holt, and our other MBV project organizations.

Managing By Values can and does make a difference. I invite you to join Michael and me on this Managing By Values journey. The story, written with the help of Jim Ballard, depicts the transformation your organization could undergo and how you can make a difference in the lives of your people, the customers you serve, and the shareholders who depend on your success. Welcome to the Fortunate 500 journey!

*Ken Blanchard*
*Fall 1996*

# I

# Finding Out

TOM YEOMANS DROVE his silver Lexus off the
freeway two exits before the one he always used
on his way home from work. He followed a winding
country road for a mile or so to where a short,
unpaved road took him into a stand of trees on a rise
overlooking a bend in a wide river. He stopped the car
and switched off the engine. He got out, walked a few
paces, then stood gazing downriver. Even with
designer sunglasses shading his eyes against the late
afternoon sun, you could see that he wore the look of
a troubled man.

Tom Yeomans' life was outwardly impressive. He'd
become president and CEO of a top manufacturing
company before the age of forty. The highly profitable
company was a leader in its field and occupied a
respected role in the community. Tom had a fine home
and a wife and children who would make any man

proud. Outwardly, his life did not seem to lack for any comforts or possessions.

It was an outcome of a pattern of ceaseless striving. His whole life had been a matter of setting and achieving goals. He was now at a point most people would call the "pinnacle of success," yet he felt strangely empty, cut off from the kinds of things he sensed made a man really rich. The plain fact was Tom wasn't happy.

He picked up a stone and threw it into the water. As he gazed at the widening ripples, his thoughts traveled back to a decade ago when he and Barry Lofting had founded L&Y Manufacturing, a successful furniture manufacturer. The two had been friends since junior high school and had worked night and day to craft L&Y into a leader in its field.

They'd had a ball doing it, too. Their success was due in part to their differences. Tom enjoyed the part of the "high roller," thriving on the risks of wheeling and dealing. Barry exuded a human intelligence demonstrated by his natural talent for establishing trust and rapport with clients and employees. The trouble had come when Tom went behind Barry's back to sell the company to a foreign buyer. Barry had never forgiven Tom for that.

Tom tried repeatedly to placate his partner's feelings. "Hey, what are you squawking about?" he'd say. "You're rich!" His efforts hadn't worked. It was only when he had tried unsuccessfully to interest his friend in going in with him on a new venture that Tom had realized money was not the real issue.

Now, as he stood looking downriver, Tom's mind was replaying that last uncomfortable conversation before Barry left the office.

"Come on, Barry. I need you. We can do it—the old fire, man. Just stick with me for two years. Sure, it may mean twelve- and fourteen-hour days for us, but we'll be having a blast blowing the competition away, and besides, it's only for a little while. Guaranteed, we'll triple our investment in that time. Then you and I will get that place in Baja and spend the time we want with our wives and kids."

Barry had looked at him steadily. "Tom, tell me something honestly."

"Anything, pal."

"When is the last time you and Leslie and the kids did anything together?" The silence between them had seemed to push the walls back.

"When is the last time you and Leslie had a real talk?" Again that maddening silence. "I thought so. Hey, I gotta go," Barry sighed. As he reached the door, he turned, looked at Tom directly, and said, "The trouble with you, Tom, is that *you're in a rat race. Remember, even if you win the race, you're still a rat.*"

That was the last time Tom saw the man he'd called his best friend—the person with whom he'd won high school swim team trophies, scaled peaks in Alaska, and built a successful business. After that,

Tom dropped the notion of starting another company and instead used his track record and contacts to join RimCo, a growing auto parts manufacturer, as a regional vice president.

The ensuing years found him competing in a grueling succession of power moves as he scaled RimCo's corporate ladder. Now, having attained the top rung as president, Tom was beginning to wonder what he'd given up. Keeping a schedule of long hours, late meetings, and frequent traveling had kept him from being a real member of his family. Leslie complained that the kids were growing up without him.

He thought of Leslie. When they spoke, it was usually to coordinate their schedules; they seldom even went to bed at the same time now. He thought of his children. Just last week he'd arrived home late at night after three days of back-to-back strategy meetings on the road. The next morning Michael, his fourteen-year-old, had come into the bedroom to kiss his mother before going off to school. Leslie, in her usual motherly attempt at building family togetherness, nudged her son, "Hey, don't you say 'hi' to your dad anymore? He's missed you while he was gone." Michael, in his sunny innocence, replied, "Oh! Were you gone again, Dad?"

Tom Yeomans turned and walked back to his sleek, silver automobile. He put his hands on the hood and leaned down over it. Reflected in the creamy wax finish he saw a face lined with suffering. As he studied that face, it spoke to him. "How about it, Tom? Do your loved ones think you're a rat?" Turning and leaning against the hood, he folded his arms and shivered in the breeze picking up off the water. The truth was, the state of his relationships at home was only the tip of the iceberg.

During the last six months at work, the ground had begun to cave in under him. Everything seemed to be coming apart. The company had lost two major accounts to its chief competitor. Complaints from customers had increased. Stockholders were getting edgy about the loss of market share. And employee morale was taking a nosedive. Some of the company's best people had quit.

Alarmed, the board of directors called in a consulting group to study the situation. Tom was concerned about outsiders snooping around, but the board gave him no choice.

The consultants used interviews, surveys, focus groups, and document reviews to put together an in-depth analysis of the company, its management, employees, stockholders, and customers. When the study was finished, the board had an all-day meeting with Lynn, the consulting team leader. Tom sat sullenly, listening to the team's list of recommendations.

The list was formidable. Tom had always thought he was out in front of the pack. But as he listened, he recognized that RimCo's problems were no different from the problems other organizations were experiencing in the highly competitive market of the nineties. The consultants suggested that the organization must be leaner, flatter. Managers must empower their people, delegating whole projects to self-managing work teams. Quality and service must become everyone's business, regardless of job title. In short, the company must "reinvent" itself from the top down.

Typically, Tom assumed that the problem was "out there." His mind began to flash with ideas about fixing "them." It was at that point that Lynn's feedback started to hit closer to home.

As she finished summarizing the results of an employee survey, Lynn put down her papers. She looked at Tom and said, "What they're saying, Mr. Yeomans, is that you manage more by fear than by consensus. Your management style breeds these problems, for it has resulted in an environment of mistrust. Without a dramatic change on your part, it will be difficult, if not impossible, for RimCo to become a really competitive company for the long term."

Well, there it was. It seemed Barry's prediction had come true. Tom's own people thought he was a rat.

The sun was sinking as Tom Yeomans climbed behind the wheel of his car and started the engine. He sat there, hands on the wheel, thinking. Then he drove off.

Even before he reached home, Tom felt that something in him had changed, that back there on the riverbank a certain clarity had started to set in.

When he got home, he did something he'd never done before—he sat down and watched cartoons with his seven-year-old daughter, Peg. From the way she snuggled up to him and stroked his hand he could tell that Peg, who was usually the "odd one out" when her older brothers got together, liked the attention. But the real recipient of the affection was Dad.

Later, when Leslie drove up, she found Tom shooting baskets with the boys in the driveway. After greeting her, Tom helped Leslie carry the groceries in from the car.

The phone rang as they were putting the groceries away. It was Fran, Tom's assistant. "I hope you're planning to attend your service club meeting tonight. Jim Wheeler was scheduled to introduce the speaker, but he's not feeling well. He wondered if you'd stand in for him."

"Well, um, okay. Looks like they need me."

"You mean you'll do it?"

"Sure."

"Great! The speaker you'll be introducing is Jack Cunningham. I'll fax the background notes on him to you right away."

"Okay. Thanks, Fran," Tom said.

There was a pause on the line. Then Fran asked, "Mr. Yeomans, are you all right?"

"Sure. Why do you ask?"

"Oh, I'm just kind of surprised that you'd do it."

"No problem, Fran. Really. Send the fax."

Reading Jim Wheeler's notes, Tom noted the title of Cunningham's speech, "The Journey of the Fortunate 500," and smiled at the play on words. He reviewed some brief background facts on the man and his clients, then turned to the key points to be used in the introduction. One item caught Tom's attention—it read: "Many executives claim Jack Cunningham has not only helped them change their companies but has impacted their personal lives as well." Tom was pondering this as Leslie came into the room.

He turned to her suddenly. "Honey, would you go with me tonight to my club meeting? I'd like you to be there when I introduce the speaker, and then, on the way home, we can talk about the things we heard him say."

Leslie's quick smile evidenced her pleasure. "That suits me fine," she glowed.

# II

# The Acts of Life

H E DIDN'T REMEMBER much about getting to the meeting, or even about introducing the featured speaker. But once seated in the front row next to Leslie, Tom gave Jack Cunningham's words his full attention.

Something about this man appealed to Tom. It almost seemed as if Cunningham was speaking directly to him.

Shortly into his talk, Jack Cunningham remarked, "In all my travels, I've found a number of people who appear outwardly successful but who are actually inwardly unhappy and unfulfilled. They may appear to have it all together, but they really feel empty inside." Tom could feel his attention lock onto the speaker as he continued, "Now this realization can be painful, but the fact is, it's a wake-up call."

Cunningham went over to a flip chart and uncovered a sign that read:

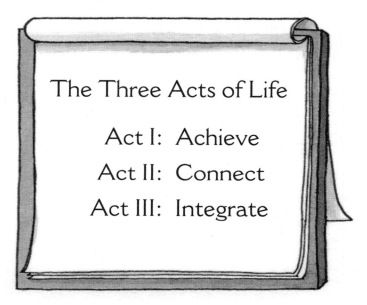

The Three Acts of Life

Act I:   Achieve

Act II:   Connect

Act III:   Integrate

"There are three acts in life," he resumed. "Act One is *Achieve*. Achieving is a natural act for human beings. We may be the only species able to set goals beyond day-to-day survival, so it's very natural for us to want to achieve—to want to *be* something. Act One is about being-by-doing.

"Many people think that Achieve is the only act in town. They're always looking for the next victory, the next sale, or the next conquest. But I've never heard of anyone on their deathbed who said, 'I wish I'd gone to the office more.'"

As Tom chuckled with the audience, he looked at Leslie. He could see that she, too, was enjoying the speech.

"Act Two, *Connect*, is about relationships, or being-by-being-with. During Act One, relationships are often put on the back burner. Sometimes it takes a personal crisis like financial strife, problems in one's career, or a physical illness to make a person see that what really matters in his or her life is people. Act Two involves experiencing life's menu of daily offerings, investing in your own and others' lives, and sharing your time and talents through your involvement with friends, family, and others."

As he listened to these words, Tom reflected on his own relationships at home and at work. He was starting to realize that the speaker was challenging the way he had been conducting his life. Was he stuck in Act One?

"Last comes Act Three, *Integrate*," Cunningham continued. "Integrate, or being-by-becoming, means bringing the first two acts together. It means defining or redefining your own purpose and values and then putting them into daily action in ways that are truly meaningful to you and those people, principles, and commitments you most cherish."

Jack Cunningham paused. Placing his elbows on the podium and lacing his fingers together in front of him, he leaned toward his audience with an earnest look. "It may be time for you to ask yourself, 'What is my purpose? In the larger scheme of things, what am I doing here? Has my life been about following my dream, or has it been about following somebody else's dream? Or has everything up to now been a preparation for what I've really come to do?' Only you can answer these questions. In order to do so, you often don't have to look any farther than where you are right now.

"Many of you are leaders of organizations. So even though I've been speaking on a personal level, you might need to take a look at the extent to which these questions apply equally to your organizations and groups."

The speaker paused and walked to the flip chart again. He added the phrase *Core Values*. "This matter of defining or redefining your purpose in life," he continued, "isn't just an intellectual process of arriving at a logical conclusion. You have to dig deeper, to the level of your inner values. What are the core values that, for you or your organization, will guide and shape the way you fulfill your purpose? Then, after you've identified these values, comes the toughest question: How are you demonstrating these values in your everyday dealings with the world?"

Cunningham paused again and smiled. "In this turbulent decade, many things have become confusing in business that used to be simple. American companies are busy trying simultaneously to follow lots of reasonable-sounding suggestions for surviving and gaining a competitive advantage in the global marketplace. So many new approaches are being proposed that it's no wonder they're referred to as 'flavors of the month.' Yet, in spite of much time and effort, few seem to be able to come up with an approach that will ensure success and meet the expectations of all the different groups of people involved.

"In times of constant change, it's easy for people to think that even the fundamental laws governing human decency and behavior have changed. But they haven't.

"The same kinds of basic considerations that have always been needed to keep employees committed, customers delighted, stockholders satisfied, and suppliers and creditors glad to do business with you are required now.

"An organization that can find solid footing in all its key business relationships when so many others are slipping and sliding around is indeed a fortunate one. There is a relatively simple strategy for achieving this, and already some companies are following it. Some are trying to do it on their own, by trial and error. Others are learning this plan with the help of consultants and trainers who focus on the process of aligning policies and practices. We say that those who have answered this call are undertaking *The Journey of the Fortunate 500.*"

Once again he walked over to the chart, and this time he flipped over the sheet. The new page showed a diagram that looked like this:

"This diagram shows that a Fortunate 500 organization depends on four pillars. Each pillar represents a certain group of people to whom the company has a key responsibility. We use the acronym 'CEOS' to suggest that every person associated with a Fortunate 500 organization, regardless of his or her position, needs to think, feel, and act like a leader—a kind of chief executive officer. The hope is that everyone will feel the same pride, commitment, and ownership that those in formal leadership positions do and also act in empowered ways to make the organization the best it can be. Let's look at each of these four groups.

"The letter '**C**' stands for '**C**ustomers.' The first thing that makes a Fortunate 500 organization different is the quality of service available to its customers. If you want to be competitive today, satisfying your customers isn't enough. You want customers who will brag about you—customers who will become part of your marketing and sales force. You have to treat customers in such a way that they become *raving fans* of your service.

"The letter '**E**' stands for '**E**mployees.' The second thing that makes a Fortunate 500 organization outstanding is the quality of life available to its employees. Such a company creates a motivating environment for its people—one in which employees can see that working toward the organization's goals is in their best interest. In this environment, employees begin to think like company owners. To the extent that the employees in a Fortunate 500 organization are truly treated like its most precious resource, they become more committed to its goals than are employees in other organizations where people perceive themselves as being used like expendable commodities.

"The letter '**O**' stands for '**O**wners,' or the company's stockholders. No company can be called truly fortunate unless it's profitable. But truly profitable for all stakeholder groups means being ethical. Today the trait most cited as required for effective leadership is integrity. A key point that distinguishes a Fortunate 500 organization from its competitors is the integrity of profit making and the related resource allocation practices by management and owners. So when we refer to owners, we're not talking about speculators but people who are looking for growth from a company of which they can be proud.

"The remaining pillar stands for the fourth key constituency group to which a Fortunate 500 organization is committed in a mutually beneficial business relationship. The '**S**' stands for what we call '**S**ignificant Other' groups. These may include the community, creditors, suppliers, vendors, distributors, or even respected competitors. If you're a Fortunate 500 organization, you're consciously building a spirit of shared responsibility and mutual trust between your organization and its 'significant others.'"

Jack Cunningham asked, "What holds all these pillars together? What is the lifeblood of a Fortunate 500 organization, the hallmark, the essence that binds together all of these key relationships?"

Before answering his question, Jack walked once again to his chart and flipped the page over to the next diagram, revealing a new picture that looked like this:

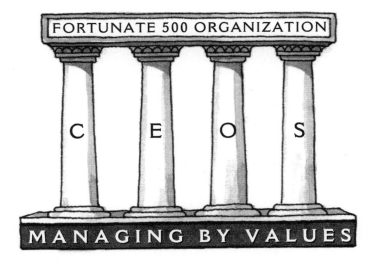

"Now our structure has a base. Today most people agree that unless companies continually demonstrate their commitment, not only to profit but also to business values like honesty, integrity, fairness, and cooperation, they are in big trouble.

"Most companies today have mission statements that seek to express their commitment to one or more of these groups. But are they actually walking their talk?

"The basis for a Fortunate 500 organization is 'Managing By Values.' It is an accepted business practice for motivating customers to keep coming back, inspiring employees to be their best every day, enabling owners to be both profitable and proud, and encouraging significant others to support their business commitments with you.

"A long time ago when I was a young boy, my grandfather used to tell me something that's always stuck in my mind. I don't know how many times he told me this, but it took root in my consciousness and I've never forgotten it. He said:

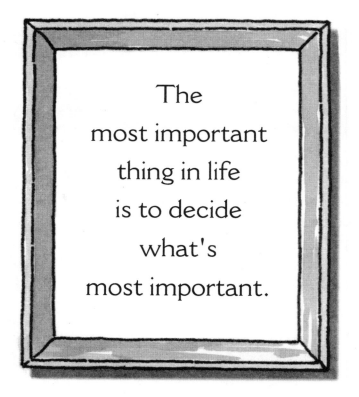

The
most important
thing in life
is to decide
what's
most important.

"If you think about it," continued Jack Cunningham, "he's absolutely right. The basis of MBV, or Managing By Values, is having your priorities straight. The way to be a Fortunate 500 organization is to have a process for making sure that your organization's values are sound and lasting. You do this by aligning both your strategic decisions and day-to-day actions with these guiding values."

Cunningham went on to say more about the process and impact of Managing By Values. As the speaker closed his talk, Tom rose with the others to applaud. Then the crowd dispersed and he headed for the podium.

"Jack, thank you for being here tonight," Tom said enthusiastically. "Could I have one of your business cards? I'd like to call you and make an appointment to talk with you about becoming a Fortunate 500 organization."

"Do you have the time to come in tomorrow morning?" Jack asked.

Tom was pleased, not expecting such a quick response. "I'll *make* the time!" he said.

As Tom and Leslie drove home, they talked about Jack Cunningham's speech. The more they talked, the more excited and supportive Leslie became about Tom's meeting the next day with Jack.

# III

# The MBV Process

Tom Yeomans arrived at Jack Cunningham's office a few minutes before ten and was shown immediately into his office. He found Jack playing with what appeared to be a white plastic box. Jack spotted Tom and came forward to welcome him.

"Greetings," he said as he shook Tom's hand warmly and motioned him to a chair. "Let's get started. I want to ask you some questions. I find in dealing with organizational leaders such as yourself, it helps to identify what I call the 'precipitating factors.' Tell me about what's been happening to you that caused you to want to explore the Managing By Values process at this time."

As Tom began talking, he found Jack Cunningham a willing audience. Before long, he was sharing his reactions to the Three Acts of Life. He said, "I saw myself right away as having pushed the limits of Act One—Achieve. Recent experiences have shown me the importance of also focusing on the other two stages, Connect and Integrate."

Tom went on to share the feedback he had received at home and at work and how it was motivating him to look at the way he related to people. He even shared the story of his traumatic breakup with his former business partner. "I see now," Tom said, "that my conflict with Barry was really about values."

"You're right," said Jack. "Your values were generated by a drive for achievement. Barry's were based on connectedness. Those we call Fortunate 500 leaders have found that a drive for success does not have to outstrip the commitment to do right by people."

Tom thought about that. Then Jack added, "I get the idea from your sadness about the breakup with Barry that your styles were compatible but your values weren't. Managing By Values often means making tough decisions, choosing the right thing over short-term focused payoffs that may be less ethical."

Tom sat up straight. "I guess that brings me to why I came to you. What can I do to enrich myself and my organization? What steps do I take to get my organization aligned around a set of core values so that I can begin this Managing By Values process?"

Jack looked at Tom for a moment before he spoke. "First of all, I think you have the order right.

You talked about changing yourself and your organization. In this work I often give people the rule of Self First. It's as important to use the process to work on yourself as it is to work on the organization."

"Are you saying that you can use Managing By Values on yourself?"

Jack nodded. "It's not that hard to figure out," he said. "It takes two things: (1) the willingness to believe in an agreed-upon set of values and (2) continuous diligence in putting those values into action."

"Diligence?"

"Diligence. A persistent focus with a lot of hard work, especially in the early stages. You must be willing to give this process time."

"How much time are we talking about?" asked Tom.

"It takes about two or three years for this change process to really start taking hold and yielding consistent business returns."

"I guess Managing By Values is no quick fix," Tom replied.

"Right," said Jack. "And it takes just as long for lasting changes to take place in a person's behavior. That's important to remember because people are where the action is." He turned and pointed to a plaque on the wall of his office. Tom read:

> Organizations
> don't make
> Managing By Values
> work.
> People do!

"The reason Managing By Values works," Jack said, "is that valuing is a *people* process."

Jack picked up the white box he'd been toying with when Tom walked in. Placing it on the desk in front of Tom, he said, "Take a look at this."

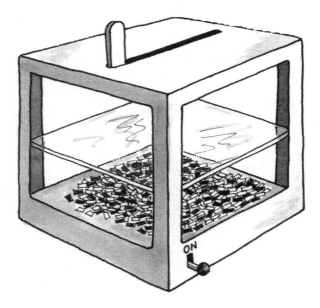

"It looks interesting," said Tom. "What is it?"

"It's an idea I came up with to demonstrate MBV for clients and interested associates," Jack answered. "I call it the 'Alignment Puzzle.'"

Tom picked up the smooth plastic cube and examined it. It was about five inches square and had clear plastic windows for sides. Noting a tiny power switch on one side, he concluded that the object was battery powered. Tom brought the cube closer to his face and peered into it.

A clear plastic sheet divided the window sections horizontally, like a see-through ceiling. He saw that the floor of the space below the ceiling was covered with a collection of tiny rectangular flakes, some red and some blue.

As he shook the box, the flakes moved around and spilled over each other in random fashion. On top of the box was a lever set into a groove that ran the length of the cover.

Fascinated, Tom glanced at Jack, who had come around and was sitting on the desk. Jack smiled and nodded as if to say, "Go ahead."

Tom set the box down on the desk and flipped the power switch to the "on" position. Then, holding the base with one hand, he began to move the lever slowly in its groove across the top. As he did so, his eyes widened and his mouth opened in amazement.

Quite literally, the effect was electrifying. As the lever moved over them, the colored flakes on the floor jumped up to the horizontal ceiling and arranged themselves into a colored pattern. They spelled out a message:

"Wow! How did it *do* that?" Tom asked.

"How do you think?" laughed Jack, fully satisfied with Tom's reaction.

"Well, I have a hunch—at least about part of it," Tom responded. To test his idea, he switched the power off. Immediately, all the colored flakes dropped away to the floor in a disarranged heap, looking as they had before, like a fragmented collection of confetti. Tom looked at Jack and said, "I remember enough high school physics to be able to figure out the basic principle. Electromagnetism, right?"

Jack nodded approvingly. "Okay," Tom continued, "the batteries in the base send a current to a magnet under the operating lever. These colored chips are made of iron or some other magnetic metal. As the magnet passes over the chips, it attracts and aligns them. They snap up onto this glass sheet and . . ." Tom paused and looked perplexed. "But how the heck do the two kinds of colors distribute themselves to form this MBV sign?"

"Aha!" exclaimed Jack, smacking his hands together in delight. "That's the important question!"

Tom could tell that Jack Cunningham wasn't about to reveal the answer right away. He settled back in his chair, looked at Jack, and surrendered a sigh.

"All right, Jack," he said, taking out his notebook and pen, "You've got my attention! I suppose this Alignment Puzzle is related to the subject of Managing By Values. Right?"

Jack grinned. "How do you suppose it could demonstrate the processes used in undertaking that journey?"

Tom leaned forward so that his face was level with the white box. He spent a few moments playing with the mechanism, turning on the power switch and moving the control lever back and forth to see how the chips arranged themselves in flawless response to the magnet. "Could you give me a little hint?" he asked.

Jack reached over to turn the power switch to "off." As before, the colored flakes immediately fell to the bottom. "See all those random red and blue pieces lying there pointing every which way? How long do you think it would take for you to arrange all of them into the MBV pattern by hand, without using the electromagnet?"

Tom thought a moment. "Hmm. Using a magnifying glass and some tweezers, if I worked for about five hours I might be able to glue all of those flakes to the underside of that glass."

"Doesn't sound like much fun to me."

"No fun at all. It would be painstaking, tedious work. My eyesight and patience would probably be exhausted in the process. And even if I did succeed in gluing them in place, the whole dynamic of the box would be lost."

Jack nodded. "Now let's compare managing particles to managing people and organizations," he said. "Suppose you want to get a company of individuals all going in the same direction to accomplish your organizational goals. You know how difficult alignment is to accomplish, considering the variety of needs, values, and expectations people have, right?"

Thinking of his own team at RimCo, Tom nodded. "Not only is it difficult and no fun at all, but it just doesn't work. I know many managers who have burned out on that very task, and their organizations are no further ahead than when they started." Tom sat quietly for a moment, staring at the box on Jack's desk.

Then he straightened up with sudden energy and stared at Jack. "Wait a minute," he said. "I think I know what this is about."

Jack only smiled his enigmatic smile.

"MBV . . . Managing By Values. That's it, isn't it?" Tom asked.

Jack Cunningham smiled again. "It's values that align people, that get them all committed to working for common goals," Tom exclaimed.

With that he reached forward to the white box and threw the control lever all the way to "on." "What it's saying is that MBV is the ultimate human attractor that acts like this magnet. Values are the only phenomena that can be moved across a group of people so that they become aligned like these chips."

"That's the idea," Jack said.

"But how do you go about Managing By Values?" Tom wanted to know. "Are there some specific steps?"

"I thought you'd never ask," Jack said, reaching toward a small stand-up frame on his desk. He turned it around so that it faced Tom. Tom read:

The MBV Process

Phase 1: *Clarifying* our mission/purpose and values

Phase 2: *Communicating* our mission and values

Phase 3: *Aligning* our daily practices with our mission and values

Tom was about to copy down the steps when Jack picked up the sign and handed it to him.

"For me?" Tom said, surprised. Jack nodded.

Tom asked, "Where can I learn more about this MBV process? Are there some organizations I could read about and visit with that have already implemented it?"

"I like people who anticipate what I'm about to tell them," said Jack. He handed two cards to Tom. Each card bore the name, address, and phone number of a contact person at a well-respected company.

"I suggest you visit these places right away. Start with Telecom Distributors. Arlene Whalen, chief financial officer there, will help you get a sense of how the first two phases operate. I took the liberty of phoning Arlene to set up an appointment. She told me she can see you at 11:30, if that's okay." Tom nodded enthusiastically.

"When you make your other visit," Jack said as he walked Tom to the office door, "you'll learn about the third phase. Alexa Montague over at Meredith Manufacturing is expecting you at 9:30 tomorrow morning."

Tom was thrilled. "Thanks," he said, shaking Jack's hand emphatically. "You've given me a lot to think about."

"My pleasure," said Jack Cunningham. He picked up a container from a stack on a shelf by the door and handed it to Tom. From its size and shape, Tom guessed it held another Alignment Puzzle. "Don't forget this," Jack smiled. "You might find it an inspirational reminder."

*    *    *

As Tom Yeomans drove to Telecom, he could hardly believe that his inquiry about MBV was rolling along so quickly and smoothly. He felt like he had linked into a fortunate stream of new resources.

As he thought about what had transpired in less than twenty-four hours, Tom suddenly remembered a card Leslie had given him several weeks before. He had read it hastily and slipped it into his wallet. Now, pulling up to a stoplight, Tom got out his wallet and took out the card. An indescribable feeling spread through him as he read it.

## The moment one commits, Providence acts, too.

–Goethe

# IV

# The Search Begins

A T ELEVEN-THIRTY sharp, Tom was in the waiting room outside an executive office at Telecom Distributors, a large, well-known communications equipment and service provider.

A tall woman emerged from the office and walked briskly toward him, extending her hand. "Hi, Tom! I'm Arlene Whalen," she announced. "Come on in."

Once they were seated in her office, Arlene said, "So, you've been talking to Jack Cunningham, eh? I bet you have an Alignment Puzzle in your car right now."

Tom grinned and nodded. He was glad to be starting with someone on the "hard" side of the business. "Arlene, with your background in number crunching, I'm sure you can tell me—does this Managing By Values really work in the business world?"

Arlene Whalen smiled. "I've got to confess, when I first heard our CEO presenting the idea to us, I thought it was just another fad. But I'm happy to report that MBV has turned me around, as well as our organization."

"How do you mean?"

"MBV is all about identifying gaps between what you say you believe and how you actually perform. For example, many companies talk a good service game, but they don't walk it. Some managers claim they have an open-door policy, but try and get in to see them.

"Three years ago, when we started working with Jack to implement MBV, we went through a process of articulating our values. Jack asked us, 'By what values do you want to be known? How do you want your customers and your employees to feel toward the company?' We came up with three great values, that have focused our MBV alignment process." Arlene pointed to a sign on the wall:

1. Be ETHICAL
2. Be RESPONSIVE
3. Be PROFITABLE

"Now," she continued, "you'd think that someone in my position would place these values in reverse order, right?"

"Right."

"Actually, the MBV process has taught all of us that precisely this ordering of our espoused values is critically important. But let's deal with 'profitable' first anyhow, as a way of reviewing bottom-line results. We had the typical slow MBV start-up because, as usual, it takes time for people to become aligned around values. But by the end of the second year of our MBV journey, results began to show on the bottom line. Sales were up 15 percent and profits were 10 percent beyond our budget estimates. And these trends have continued. We're attracting new customers and keeping customers we used to lose.

"The same is happening with our employees. Our employee turnover has decreased steadily as we've moved forward on the journey."

"That's impressive!" exclaimed Tom. "It sounds like your 'MBV journey,' as you call it, has been profitable all around."

"As we say, it's made both dollars and sense. But I don't want you to think it's been without its difficulties," Arlene cautioned.

"You mean nobody just waved a magic wand?"

"Anything but," Arlene explained. "Telecom, as you probably know, was well known and financially strong for years. But as we got into this decade, it turned out we were one of those companies that was caught resting on its laurels. Stability is desirable, but so is financial performance. We knew our return to our stockholders was growing, but we had to wake up to the fact that it was clearly below the industry average."

"Hmm. What was the reason?"

"Like many companies in these times, it wasn't obvious to us at first. It had to do with something we'd been neglecting—our relationships. For example, we thought our customers were satisfied—until we lost some of them to smaller start-up competitors with innovative ideas.

"It was the same story with our workforce. We were starting to lose some of our best people. I hate to think what would have happened if we hadn't taken action through MBV."

"I'm puzzled," said Tom. "How can a 'soft' appearing process like Managing By Values be responsible for such a turnaround in today's tough, bottom-line times?"

"Success in our business is all about service," replied Arlene. "It's true that if we don't have a high-quality product, we're not likely to survive the numbers game, and the pricing still has to be right. Nonetheless, quality and price are default items today in our business. They just give us access to the playing field.

"Service is where we gain our edge, and service means people—it's about our relationships. Customers and employees are the two critical groups. Nowadays, if we're not walking our talk with our customers and employees, we might be walking to bankruptcy court. It's happened to more than one of our competitors."

"Okay," said Tom, "that takes care of the 'C's and the 'E's in '**CEOS**.'"

"Exactly. As far as the 'O's—our 'Owners'—are concerned, they are delighted with the fact that we're now among the top five rated companies in our industry for investors.

"And our relationships with the 'S's—our 'Significant Others'—is a point of pride all around. Many of us, of course, have children in the local schools. About the same time we began our values journey as a company, we found there was considerable concern among parents and community members regarding 'character education.'

"Our company responded to this concern by sponsoring a program in our schools called 'Ethical Leadership: Now and Tomorrow.' Not only has the company's standing in the community been enhanced," insisted Arlene, "but we've now hired six high school graduates who have been through the curriculum. I can also report that our supplier relationships have improved through MBV.

"As a result of aligning with and living by our values, we've seen decreases in legal costs, unemployment insurance rates, workers' compensation, EEO complaints, and the number of wage disputes. This improvement has even occurred in locations where there's been a significant recession. That's pretty important to a career financial type like me."

Tom noticed that Arlene had an MBV desk sign like the one Jack had given him. Pointing to it, he said, "Jack told me that during my visit here I would probably also come to understand what's involved in the first two phases of the MBV process—clarifying and communicating the mission and values."

Arlene nodded. "For that, I want you to meet with our CEO, Ed Eastland. Ed wanted you to start with me to give you the bottom-line results. He does that to whet a person's appetite for the actual 'how-to' information. Let's walk over to Ed's office."

On the way, Tom thanked Arlene for filling him in on the bottom-line issues. "I have those issues in a new perspective now," Tom said. "I remember hearing Jack Cunningham talk about them in terms of tennis. He asked us what kind of performance we thought tennis players would have if instead of keeping both eyes on the ball, they always had an eye on the scoreboard. I thought that was an excellent comparison."

Arlene was familiar with the analogy. She said, "In sports, they talk about being in the 'zone.' The harder athletes try to win, the less likely they are to find their zone. When people are in the zone, all of their attention is on what they're doing, not on what they're accomplishing. The results just seem to flow from this focus of energy and competence. Lots of companies seem to watch only their scoreboard—the bottom line. In doing so, they take their eyes off the ball—their relationships with people. That gets them out of the zone and invites long-term disaster.

"Over these past three years, I've gained both increasing confidence in and, yes, genuine commitment to the priority of our values—first being *Ethical*, then *Responsive*, then *Profitable*. When we keep our eyes on consistently operating our business by aligning with our core values, the scoreboard does in fact take care of itself!"

# V

# Clarifying Your Mission and Values:

## Phase 1 of the MBV Process

$S$ OON ARLENE WAS introducing Tom to the chief executive officer. "Tom Yeomans, I want you to meet Ed Eastland, our CEO." Tom shook hands with a big, hearty man who made him feel at ease immediately. Arlene excused herself, and the two company heads sat down in Ed's office.

Tom told his story to Ed and added, "I guess my first question is, how do I go about clarifying my company's mission and values?"

Ed got right to the point. "First of all, you have to get approval from the company's owners or board to begin this process. Once you have that, you need to decide what key values you want to drive your business strategy and tactics and their order of priority. You also need to define your company's mission. If your company already has a mission statement, you'll need to determine whether it reflects the values you've identified. If not, you'll need to revise it to be consistent with those values."

"That doesn't sound too difficult," said Tom, taking notes as Ed spoke.

"It's not, but it may take time. You need to let those values percolate. Sometimes you think you have this set straight, and suddenly a really vital clarification is made by someone and you're surprised you could have left it out. It's a good idea to let this list flow at first, then come back to revise it later.

"In addition to ensuring that the list of values represents *the* values by which you want to be known and operate," continued Ed, "you have to make the values clear. The more simple, direct, and easy to understand they are, the better. Your mission and values statements should also align with the company's vision. They should be viewed as a way to energize your company's business and ensure its future well-being."

"Your company's list of values certainly seems to pass the test," said Tom. "What's next?"

"Once you are satisfied with your own version of the statements, it's time to involve your top management team."

"What do you mean, involve them?" Tom said, looking worried.

Ed stopped and looked intently at his visitor. "Tom," he said pointedly, "you've got to understand that values are not done *to* people but *with* them. This is a collaborative process. As CEO, you're like a writer—you write the first draft, but lots of editors take over after that. The members of your top management team are your first editors.

"Since you want them to be able to express themselves freely, I'd recommend you not be at their first meeting. You might do what I did and bring in an outside consultant like Jack Cunningham to facilitate the group's coming up with its own list of recommended values. That way you reduce any potential reluctance to be open that may be created by your presence. You don't want members of your management team to feel they have to agree with your views just because you're the boss. You want them to think and state their ideas freely."

"Hmm," reflected Tom, "I can see the advantage of using objective outside help here. I've found out recently that people see me as managing by fear rather than by consensus, so I guess I might really intimidate my top management team if I were to participate in their values-generation meeting. To be honest, though, if I were left out of that first meeting, I'd wonder if they might gang up on me."

"That's understandable," replied Ed. "What's important is to minimize top-down decision making about the values. After your top managers share their perceptions, you'll rejoin them to compare their views with yours."

"Now," said Tom, shifting uncomfortably, "what happens if their perceptions are different from mine?"

Ed nodded. "That's not a tragedy, but it is important information. The point is, the process is not about you or any one person—it's about what's best for the company."

Ed paused a moment and then reiterated his point. "In Managing By Values, we say that *the real 'boss' is the company's adopted values.* That's the authority we all must serve."

Tom thought for a moment and then wrote something in his notes. He leaned forward and showed it to Ed.

> In a company that
> truly manages by its
> values, there is only
> one boss—
> the company's values.

"That's an intriguing concept," Tom said
thoughtfully.

"I'm glad you think so," Ed smiled. "There's
something good in people that is brought out when
they pool their energies to serve something bigger.
Values, provided people have had the opportunity to
'elect' them, can be such a master. Shared values can
become the basis for decision making. Everything
from what software provider to go with, to how a
conflict in a work-team meeting should be handled, to
whether or not to take the company public is referred
to the new 'boss' for answers.

"In fact," Ed added, pointing to a wall poster,
"that's our sort of fun idea of an organization chart."

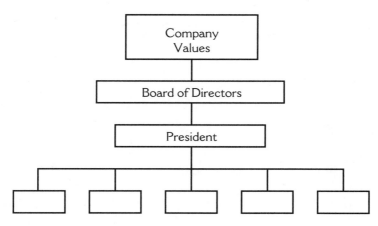

Rest of the Organization

Ed continued, "Once you and your top management group have agreed on your company's mission and a set of prioritized values, it's time to find out what the people throughout your company think. We had Jack Cunningham hold a series of focus groups with a representative sampling of employees from all levels and areas of our organization. At these meetings, Jack got input from 'the troops' regarding our draft mission and values statement to see if they believed these were in the best interest of the company—and themselves."

"So, this is where you find out whether your people are willing to 'sign up' and get behind the mission and values," said Tom.

"Exactly. It's important to make sure that people truly understand what the values mean. If there's a problem with the set of described values, we use these meetings to get suggestions about improving it. If they suggest additional key values, these are considered as well. We're also interested in feedback as to how the values should be prioritized."

"Hmm," Tom mused. "I hear you saying to involve everyone this way, but it's sure not the way I'm used to doing things. Frankly, I'm afraid people will screw things up."

Ed nodded. "A familiar fear. I was used to handling these things as executive decisions myself. But even though I kept tight hold on the reins, morale and market share still went down. What's been your experience?"

Tom hung his head. "Exactly the same," he murmured. "So what's next?"

"Next," Ed continued, "you have to determine whether your employees are genuinely enthusiastic about their company's mission and values. Unless they can link them to their actual work lives, they're meaningless. They need to answer questions like these:

- "Do they see the mission and values as guidelines they can identify with to sustain pride in the company?
- "Do the mission and values truly provide a basis for daily communications and decision making throughout the organization?
- "Do the mission and values provide a new set of rules of the road for allocating resources and solving task and people problems?"

"How many focus groups do you hold?" Tom asked.

"That depends on the size of your workforce and whether the employees' buy-in requires the involvement of everyone or just a representative sampling. The rule of thumb is to include both likely supporters and possible detractors. Once you collect and collate their feedback, you refine your mission and values accordingly. If the employees have suggested any significant changes—for instance, a reprioritizing of values—it will really make a difference to them when these suggestions are reflected in the final statements."

Tom's discomfort was growing. He was not prepared for the shift in his own role as leader that this man was describing. He tried to keep his voice steady. "Are there any other people involved?"

"Yep! Once you've made revisions based on employee feedback, you're ready to make final checks with customers and significant others such as the community, industry leaders, and key suppliers. You can do this through phone interviews or focus groups, asking questions like, 'How would this mission and these values affect the continuation of your business with us?' or 'Do such principles really make a significant difference in deciding whom you do business with?'"

"Do customers readily participate and give you feedback?"

"Sure," said Ed.

"After getting all this input, what do you do with it?" Tom asked.

"You have to synthesize it. Then it's ready for you to run it past the board—if you have one. Getting my own board's buy-in—particularly its executive committee-—was key because I needed its support in dealing with speculators who could care less about whether a company manages by values. The only concern of speculators is whether stock prices increase daily. Our price has surely risen in recent years, but MBV is a long-term growth strategy, not a quick fix to impress Wall Street while risking the company's future in the process."

All of the time Ed had been explaining the process of clarifying values, Tom had continued to jot things down in his notebook. "Let's see if I've got this straight now," he said as he read the following notes to Ed:

---

**PROCESS FOR
CLARIFYING VALUES**

1. Get owner's approval of MBV process.
2. CEO provides own input about the values.
3. Management team provides input without CEO.
4. CEO and top management team share and compare.
5. Employee focus groups provide input.
6. Check with customers and significant others.
7. Synthesize all inputs and present recommended mission/values to board of directors/owners for final approval.

---

"You're a quick study," Ed said, with a wink.

Tom was looking troubled, however. He said, "Being in the top post like you are, I'm wondering about my own commitment of time and effort. It sounds like Managing By Values is a pretty important part of your job."

Ed smiled. "Tom, Managing By Values *is* my job. MBV is not a program. It's not an add-on. Managing By Values is the way our company lives. It's everything we do. And you're right—it won't happen in your company if you don't see it that way and if you're not vitally committed to it.

"Success in this process is all about the CEO and other top leaders walking the values talk, particularly during the initial period of the journey. In the beginning, as the leader, it is your job to focus the energy and resources of the company as people start to come aboard. Then you can gradually become more of a co-participant and even a cheerleader as others throughout the company internalize the journey. All stakeholders must know that you are 100 percent committed to the benefits provided them by the company's new way of life."

"Makes sense," Tom said thoughtfully as he wrote in his notebook. His tone showed that he was mulling over this crucial leadership commitment.

"You're not sold on all this, are you?" Ed asked. "Did Jack tell you about his rule?"

"What rule is that?" asked Tom.

"Self First."

"Oh, yeah. That's the idea that *you* have to change before you can change the organization. Well, I can see I've got changing to do, all right."

Tom felt he was revisiting an old place in himself, and it didn't feel good. Hearing Jack's speech the other evening had jump-started him. And visiting Jack in his office had given him hope—Managing By Values might really be the answer for bringing RimCo out of its slump. But now he was disillusioned. It wasn't going to be as grand and easy as he'd imagined—not by a long shot. He'd hit the wall. MBV had brought him to another discomforting face-off with himself.

"Thank you, Ed, very much," Tom said. "I think I've got a pretty good handle on Phase One of the process—*clarifying* your company's mission and values.

Now I'm ready to learn more about Phase Two—
*communicating* your mission and values."

# VI

# Communicating:
## Phase II of the MBV Process

I F YOU'RE READY to hear about Phase Two, the *communicating* phase of Managing By Values," said Ed, picking up the phone, "I'd like you to talk with Maria Gonzales, our director of human resources. She's been our internal coordinator for the communicating phase."

In a few minutes, Maria Gonzales showed up. Maria's intense dark eyes and brisk manner let Tom know she was focused on business.

"So you want to know how to communicate your mission and values in ways that fit into real agendas for your business and employees?" Maria asked as they walked toward a lounge area. Tom nodded in assent.

"Your company operates primarily in four states and has about twelve hundred employees, so I'd say the communications process might best be launched by holding kickoff meetings at each of your sites, Tom."

Tom was impressed by Maria's grasp of his situation. They helped themselves to some coffee and sat down at a table. "How would you handle these meetings?" he asked.

"At our own kickoff meetings we brought in Jack Cunningham to share the speaking platform with Ed. Jack led off the meetings by telling everybody what the Fortunate 500 journey of Managing By Values was all about. He captured the audience right away using stories to illustrate how this process could change our company, our work groups, and our personal lives.

"After that, Ed spoke to us. What he said showed that his own commitment to the MBV process was absolute and unwavering. When he reviewed the seven steps that had been used for gaining input from everybody, we could see that the values were ours, not just his. He showed slides of our company's adopted mission statement and core business values, and he went over the statements. He explained the vision behind Telecom's commitment to this Fortunate 500 journey and what everyone was expected to do to put the mission and values into daily practice at work.

"He emphasized that implementing the MBV process well would create a better future for all. Then came an important step. Ed decided on a dramatic way to deliver this message through his own actions. He announced that as a result of employee feedback on perceived hierarchical roles, he was beginning a campaign of doing away with what he called 'symbols of inequality.' To live up to our Ethical value there would be no more executive parking spaces or washrooms. Everyone in the company was from that moment on to be referred to as an 'associate,' rather than by a formal title.

"To bring this home, Ed stuck a big name tag on his chest, saying 'Ed Eastland, Associate.' He had helpers pass out similar name tags with 'Associate' printed at the bottom and asked the audience to write their names on them and wear them."

Tom smiled. "He was not just telling them, he was showing them."

"Right," Maria replied. "Other companies might not go for this dramatic a move, but it turned out to be important for us."

At the close of the meeting, everyone received a laminated copy of the mission statement and key values, a guide for putting them into daily action on the job, and a copy of the company's implementation plan for their integration into our business and daily lives over the next three years."

Maria pointed to two framed posters on the wall near where they were sitting.

As Tom read the posters, he was impressed with the evident care that had gone into formulating them. "I notice," he said, "that each of your operating values is further defined in terms of each of the company's key stakeholder groups—your CEOS—Customers, Employees, Owners (shareholders), and Significant Others, in your case, the community."

---

## OUR OPERATING VALUES

### 1. ETHICAL

- Conduct our business fairly and with integrity both with customers and in the marketplace.
- Ensure fair and equitable treatment of employees.
- Provide complete and accurate information for shareholders.
- Provide leadership and practice our values in the community.

### 2. RESPONSIVE

- Identify customer expectations and deliver on commitments in a timely manner.
- Demonstrate respect for all employees and their ideas.
- Deliver on commitments to shareholders.
- Encourage employee participation in community service.

### 3. PROFITABLE

- Provide cost-effective, technologically superior products for customers.
- Encourage personal initiative and opportunity for employees.
- Produce a reasonable return on equity for shareholders.
- Make contributions that strengthen the community.

---

"Yes," said Maria. "It was an option we selected that seemed to fit best for our situation, though many companies prefer to define their values in ways that fit for all their key stakeholders.

"The posters and desk cards you see all around the place," continued Maria, "are to make sure that everyone has a basic awareness of our mission and values. They function as attitude- and behavior-shaping tools. When the mission and values are constantly kept in front of people, these tools have a better chance of doing what they were created to do—focus and impact our daily work practices.

"We've placed a poster in each of the areas where groups or units work as well as in any meeting rooms where key decisions are made, people congregate, or customers are received. You'll find our values displayed in the front entrance to our building, conference rooms including the board room, training rooms, and the lunch and break room areas. They're even on the back of our business cards and in our annual reports as well as company literature."

"Is there any danger of overdoing the message?" asked Tom.

"Only if you don't intend to act on these commitments," answered Maria. "In our case, everyone was involved in the formulation of our statements. These pledges are more than symbolic. They are the source of our own concept of a total quality philosophy—continuous improvement through a commitment to act on our expressed values."

"How do you get people to act on these commitments?"

"That's an alignment issue. Let me show you something, though, that not only communicates our commitment to our values but forces everyone to use them every day in their work."

Maria reached into a file folder and pulled out a sheet of paper.

"Here's a copy of what the *Guide to Values-Based Decision Making* looks like. Everyone gets a guide— either a desktop or pocket version—depending on whether their work location is in the office or the field."

---

### Guide to Values-Based Decision Making

1) Identify the value(s) and appropriate definition(s) involved in making this decision.

2) Who is directly affected by the action(s) [e.g., employees, customers, shareholders, or community]? Does it also require the involvement of others?

3) What action(s) does the appropriate value definition(s) call for in this situation [e.g., being fair and equitable to employees, delivering on commitments to shareholders]?

---

"How does this guide work?" Tom asked. "Can you give me an example?"

"Sure," said Maria. "Suppose you're trying to upgrade efficiency in one of your departments and you find that one of your long-term employees lacks computer skills. It will be time consuming and costly to bring this person up to the desired skill level, if it can be done at all. A bright, young computer whiz, now interviewing for a job, would be perfect in this position, but you don't have the resources to pay both. What do you do?"

"Exactly," said Tom. "What do you do that fits with the company's value commitments?"

"Well, using the guide, the first thing you do is identify the values involved. Looking at our operating values—Ethical, Responsive, Profitable—which would you say is most involved in this case?"

Tom thought for a moment. "I think that all of them are involved."

"Why do you say that?"

"Ethical is involved because you have to think about how you're going to treat a good employee. And since the specific concern in this situation is for department efficiency, it also involves your commitment to be Responsive to customers and Profitable for shareholders. That also implies the answer to the guide's second question: 'Who is directly affected by the action(s)?' In this case, obviously, the long-term employee, the potential new hire, and the department will all be affected by any action taken."

"Nice job, Tom. Now look at the definitions under each of these values. Do any jump out at you that could impact your decision?"

Tom read "Ensure fair and equitable treatment of *employees*" under Ethical, "Deliver on commitments to *customers* in a timely manner" under Responsive, and "Produce a reasonable return on equity for *shareholders*" under Profitable.

Maria nodded. "Where would you focus your initial energy?"

"It would have to be on Ethical," said Tom, "since that's your number one value, and the action called for in this case is first about being fair and equitable—but also about focusing on a solution that does not violate your stated commitments to other stakeholder groups. Unless, of course, you want to risk gaining trust with one stakeholder group and simultaneously losing it with the others."

Maria said, "That kind of thinking demonstrates how people actually use this practical tool. And note that it also includes determining who else you want to involve in the decision, whether you decide to replace your employee in a fair manner, train a new person in a cost-effective way, or design some other creative solution for handling this situation. In making any decision, whether it's buying or selling a division, handling a cross-departmental conflict, or something involving stakeholders, *the values have to remain the boss* for people to gain faith in them as the real source of power in the organization."

Tom sighed. "Maria," he said, "I'm going to level with you. You're talking about the values as the boss and all this collaboration, and I'm starting to see how it might work. But I feel like I've just stepped off the boat. I'm in a foreign country. Where I come from, *I've* been the boss. *I've* made all the important decisions, so I'm having a tough time with this. But I'll tell you this: Working through that example with you just now shows me there is an approach—actual tools and processes like this Guide—that is there for me to use. And that may be my salvation as I learn more about this journey. As I talk this through, I seem to be hearing the same message over and over again— change yourself first!"

"I'm glad you feel that way, Tom," Maria said thoughtfully, "because our people have told us that without tools like the *Guide to Values-Based Decision Making*, they wouldn't have a clear notion of what they are expected to do or how they are expected to do it. We want everyone to be proud of what we stand for and also to hold each other accountable for living by these beliefs.

"To us . . .

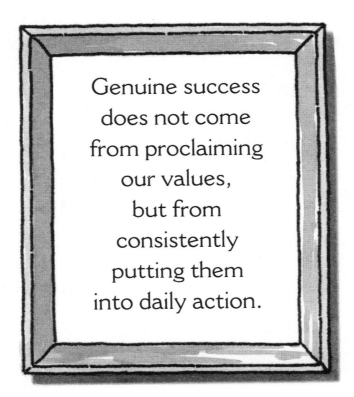

Genuine success
does not come
from proclaiming
our values,
but from
consistently
putting them
into daily action.

"That captures it," smiled Tom.

"Come with me for a moment," Maria said, getting up. "I want to show you another way we've found to communicate our mission and values."

Tom followed her down a hallway to an alcove off the main entrance to the building. There he found an entire wall devoted to a display of pictures of smiling employees. Some were individual portraits; others were photos of groups.

Below each framed picture was a caption that began with one of the key values and included a story of how that person, group, or team had consistently demonstrated that value at work. Some included unsolicited feedback from satisfied customers about how the employees had performed a service.

"We call this our *Wall of Fame*," said Maria. "This is one of the ways we share and celebrate our MBV success stories."

"What a great idea," said Tom as he scanned the Wall of Fame.

"Let's look in on a meeting here," said Maria as they continued walking down the hallway. "I've already received permission to visit."

Maria opened a door where about a dozen people were seated around a table. Several participants glanced at Maria and Tom and smiled, but the group did not seem distracted by their presence. A flip chart at the far end of the table bore the title *Success Stories*. On the table were several gold and silver certificates, each bearing the name of one of the company's three key values.

A woman was recounting to the group an anecdote about an occurrence that week in the cafeteria, where she was a supervisor. "Last Tuesday Jean discovered some spoiled tomatoes and showed them to me. Immediately I called Reynolds, our supplier. We found out the whole order was bad, and they thanked us. So I want to give Jean a plus for being 'Responsive' to her customers, the people who eat in our cafeteria and expect healthy food."

The supervisor picked up a certificate from the table and held it up for all to see. In big letters it said, "Simply the Best." She handed it to Jean, who beamed as everyone applauded.

As Maria led Tom from the room, she explained, "We begin all our meetings like that—sharing success stories about our values in action. It's another way to recognize people and to keep the values uppermost in how we work around here. We also publish selected stories in our monthly newsletter and in our annual company report."

"I can see you're serious about communicating your values," Tom enthused as they walked back toward Ed Eastland's office.

Maria agreed. "We don't ever want to hear anyone saying, 'Whatever happened to that values fad that was going around here for a while? Guess it was just another well-intentioned idea that management didn't stick with!'"

Ed listened as Tom briefly summarized the key points he had learned about Phase One—clarifying the organization's mission and values, and Phase Two—communicating the values. Ed congratulated him on his journey and told him to come back anytime and visit.

As they walked to the door, Ed said, "I guess tomorrow you'll be over at Meredith Manufacturing. Is that right?" Tom nodded. "Good. Alexa Montague and the others over at Meredith will let you know about the tough stuff."

"The tough stuff?" echoed Tom.

Ed looked earnestly at Tom. "The reason I say it's the 'tough stuff' is because it's when we're all forced to face those moments of truth and ask ourselves, 'Are we going to operate according to our values or not?' Have you read what it says on the bottom of the Alignment Puzzle Jack gave you?"

"No, I haven't," said Tom.

"Do, when you get a chance," said Ed. "It tells you why the alignment phase is worth it, even though it is tough."

Thanking his host, Tom left the building. As he headed for his car, he thought about the things he'd learned from the people at Telecom. Getting into the driver's seat, he saw the package on the seat beside him. He opened it, took out the Alignment Puzzle, and turned it over. On the bottom was a red, white, and blue sticker. It read:

When aligned
around shared
values and united in
a common mission,
ordinary people
accomplish
extraordinary
results.

# VII

# Aligning:
## Phase III of the MBV Process

A COLD RAIN was falling when Tom Yeomans arrived at the home office of Meredith Manufacturing. He was quickly escorted to the office of Alexa Montague, president and CEO of the company. Alexa was talking with a young man when Tom entered. Silver-haired but youthful appearing, the president came forward and introduced herself with a smile. "Seems we didn't order the right weather for your visit," she said. Then, turning, she added, "Tom, this is Carl Goff. He plays a major role in our alignment process. He's going to be coordinating your visit with us today."

Tom was glad when Alexa offered him a cup of coffee. The hot liquid perked his spirits. On the drive over he had been thinking about Ed Eastland's comment about Phase Three as the "tough stuff."

"I sure learned a lot in a short time at Telecom. Now I think I'm ready to learn about alignment," said Tom.

"Alignment is the heart and soul of the Managing By Values journey," explained Alexa. "Once you've clarified your mission and values and communicated them to all your key stakeholders, then it's time to focus on organizational practices and behavior to ensure they're consistent with your stated intentions, priorities, and related performance goals."

"What are Meredith's key values?" inquired Tom.

"Our number one value is the same as Telecom's. First is being *Ethical*—by doing the right thing. Then comes *Success*—by building a foundation for our survival and growth. Finally *Excellence*—by building a legacy of quality. I know that when you see a company's 'boss list' of values, it can seem like just words. What's important is the process of arriving at those values—electing those chief executives, if you will—and what those words *mean* to people when they see them or think about them."

Tom nodded. "How do you align your management practices with these values?"

"I think Carl can best explain that process. As one of our ombudspeople, he's often asked to facilitate what we call a 'Gap Reduction' plan. That's when a person or process is out of alignment with what our values intend. Why don't you and Carl start your tour now? I'll see you when you get back."

As they left the president's office, Tom said, "Alexa called you an ombudsperson. As I recall, that's an impartial mediator of some kind."

"That's right," said Carl. "It's a person who assists in conflict situations where there is a potential alignment problem. The ombudsperson's role is to ensure that the outcome of any conflict resolution effort fits with our values and, hopefully, results in mutual benefit for those involved or impacted."

"It sounds like a position of honor," said Tom. "I understand that this person is chosen by vote from people at every level throughout the company." Carl nodded. "I think congratulations are in order," Tom added.

Carl smiled modestly. "Actually, in setting up our alignment process, Alexa had everyone in the company nominate two ombudspeople, one managerial and one nonmanagerial. I'm the nonmanagement ombudsperson. I work in the regional sales department as a sales support person, but I always say I'm really in customer service. My 'customers' are our salespeople and their customers are our clients. Managing By Values has really cemented this idea of serving both internal and external customers at

Meredith. It's the heart of my work in the gap reduction process."

Tom looked thoughtful. "I understand that gap reduction is a method for creating alignment between what is intended by your mission and values and what's actually happening. How do you determine when something is out of alignment?"

"You could say it's akin to what it's like when your car's wheels are out of alignment," said Carl. "It just doesn't feel right."

"I know what you mean!" exclaimed Tom. "My car once got hit from the side. It made for a rough riding experience until I got it fixed."

"It's often the same way with problems involving people or processes in an organization. It's something you just feel," Carl said. "But to answer your question more precisely, we also use some proven measurement methods. There are three commonly used approaches to assessing whether something is out of alignment: customer satisfaction interviews and focus groups, management assessment and feedback tools, and employee surveys of the company's practices."

Tom took a moment to note these methods on his pad. "You must have gotten extensive feedback," he said.

"We did," continued Carl. "We hired an outside company to conduct the customer component."

"How'd you do on customer satisfaction?"

"We scored high on the service excellence scale—providing good service to our customers. That fits with our Success and Excellence values. We also found some gaps. One that jumped right out at us was our lack of an effective recovery strategy. Our customers said we were committed to serving them well, but when something did go wrong, we didn't respond as quickly as they expected. The feedback even located the problem for us. It told us that our service people weren't fully empowered to make decisions about how to right a wrong for a customer. Our people had been well trained to do things right the first time, but when something went wrong, they still had to check with someone up the ladder. This process slowed down their ability to be responsive."

Tom referred to the notes he'd taken. "Tell me about the management assessment and feedback tools," he said.

"That was a real change maker," Carl grinned. "Not being a senior manager myself, I didn't experience it firsthand. But everyone knows it was quite an experience for the twenty senior managers involved. It also impacted the entire company in a positive way."

"Now I'm really interested in this one," Tom said earnestly.

"The values, work styles, and adaptability patterns of managers were assessed. The process taught those folks a lot about themselves and their associates. They got anonymous feedback from both their direct reports and their peers."

"Can I talk to a manager who participated?"

"I was thinking of having you talk to 'Screamer' McGinty."

"Screamer?"

"That's a name we gave him because he was always yelling at people and putting them down."

"Does he know that everyone calls him Screamer?"

"He does now."

They headed down the hall to a corner office. Tom saw a sign on the door: *The Screamer Is In.* "It's neat when people are able to laugh at themselves like this," he said.

"It wasn't always that way," said Carl, "but I'll let Screamer tell you all about it." He knocked and they went in.

A big, hearty man glanced up and looked suddenly stern when he saw Carl. "Who's that you've got there?" he demanded.

"Bryan, meet Tom Yeomans, head man at RimCo. He's here to learn about the alignment phase of MBV. I know you're always ready to tell your Screamer story."

"Fat chance! I'm sick of being treated like an attraction at Disney. And you're one of the worst offenders, Carl."

As McGinty went into his tirade, Tom began to back away. At that, Bryan chuckled. "Sit down," he said. "I just wanted to give you a sample of my past behavior. Let me tell you about that feedback I got.

"Before the assessment, most of us managers agreed that there were certain gaps in the company all right. But we saw these gaps revolving around other people, not ourselves. Until then, I'd been sure that my own behavior exemplified the best practices according to our company's values."

Tom smiled knowingly. "I can imagine."

"Once I got over the initial shock of learning that I was known throughout the company as Screamer, I began to realize that I was part of the problem around here, not the solution."

Tom smiled. "That was a little tough on the ego, right?"

"You got that right. I can laugh about it now, but I guarantee I had a few sleepless nights in the beginning. Not only because of the feedback, but also because I realized that Alexa and everybody in the company seemed to be committed to this Managing By Values business. If I didn't get my behavior in line with our Ethical value—doing the right thing by others—career planning was going to be my only option."

"What did you do?"

"First, I agreed to attend a human interactions seminar. Working in a group of twelve people in a retreat setting gave me a look at the negative impact of my behavior firsthand. Everybody claims that most problems are caused by poor communications, right?"

"Aren't they?"

"They are and they aren't. On one hand they are, because people *aren't* communicating and being honest with each other. On the other hand, problems in organizations are often more about people's safety than about people talking to each other. In fact, we learned a rule." Bryan McGinty opened a planner that lay in front of him on the desk. Turning it, he showed Tom a reminder he'd inserted as a first page:

# Communication happens naturally when you make things safe.

"Every day when I get to work I look at this," Bryan said. "I work at making it safe for people. Because it's only through safety that trust develops, and only when there's trust can people use their interactions to achieve the purpose of human communication."

"What's that?" Tom asked.

"Mutual understanding. When I know that you and I have listened to each other and we see eye-to-eye—*then* we've communicated."

"Hmm. Does that mean we are in agreement about everything?" Tom asked warily.

"No. Communication isn't based on agreement but on understanding." Bryan paused and smiled. "So, do you get what I'm saying?"

"Got it," Tom laughed.

"Okay—just checking."

"Bryan, we've got to go," put in Carl.

"Right. Go." Bryan stood up and shook Tom's hand. "Glad we understand each other."

"Me too," laughed Tom.

"Oh, come on," Carl said. He knew that Screamer McGinty had recognized in Tom a kindred spirit.

As Tom and Carl walked down the hall, Tom summarized by saying, "So one of the toughest changes was for the people at the top. What benefit did you gain from your employee survey of company practices?"

Carl rolled his eyes on this one. "When you ask employees for their ideas on how the workplace could be improved, you've got to be ready for anything—including reluctance to speak up. Many employees felt their unit supervisors and managers were functioning in a command-and-control style. Because of this, the employees were hesitant to share their ideas and suggestions. That very reluctance of employees led us to implement targeted training and development programs in effective leadership and teamwork for managers and supervisors. We installed a feedback process that enabled managers to continually improve in these areas.

"We soon learned that one thing management could do to continue to build trust with employees was to implement quickly some of the changes they suggested. For example, in response to employee requests for more timely decision making, we changed to a decentralized branch management structure. By placing decision making closer to our customers, we also eliminated competition between several business units.

"This move empowered people and reinforced our business values of Ethical and Excellence at the same time. As a result, orders rose by 20 percent last year—in an industry where our top competitors' sales went down 10 percent—a clear example of our Success value in action."

"Would you say some more about competition between units?" Tom requested. "I have that same trouble at my company."

"Sure," said Carl. "Of course, we all know such in-house competition is very common between departments, for example, sales and marketing, production and quality, human resources and personnel, accounting and finance. It's basically a different way of seeing what separates these folks. Usually it's a clash between short-term thinking and long-term thinking. But that's a simplification, too.

Often it's the difference between types of personalities, which are hired into or otherwise find their way into these divisions according to their points of view."

"Hmm," Tom mused. "Then, once they come up against each other in the operations of the company, they clash." Carl nodded. "I'm struck by your understanding of these groups and their traditional conflicts," Tom continued. "I guess you're able to get these insights from your gap reduction work as an ombudsperson, eh?"

"Most of what you're calling insights have come from observing the way people have changed their minds over time."

"What do you mean, changed their minds?"

"One of the biggest changes I see, and the most critically useful in the MBV process, is the change from *either-or* thinking to *both-and* thinking. People are used to thinking that it's got to be *either* this way *or* that way—but it can't be both. And so both sides argue for the 'right' way as they see it. But once they start listening and admitting that the other side might have some merit, they begin to use *both-and* thinking. Then they're able to stop fighting and start collaborating. Often it takes a POPS session to work this change."

"POPS," Tom repeated. "What's that?"

"POPS stands for *People-Oriented Problem Solving*. When a situation qualifies for a POPS, it's a powerful way to use conflict to get people realigned with the company's values and with their own."

"So, values become a way to solve people problems? What do you mean by 'when a situation qualifies?'"

"Well, you don't want to use Managing By Values to slow down the company; you want to use it to make it more efficient. If you were to use POPS for every little disagreement that came up, people wouldn't get any work done. POPS is only used when an interpersonal conflict clearly is hindering the progress of a team, a department, or the company as a whole."

"How does it work?"

They stopped in front of a manager's office. Peering inside the open door, Carl said, "Let's talk to an expert. This is Sam Petrie's office. He's a manager in our service department as well as the managerial ombudsperson for the whole company, and he's been a big help to me. Sam has become quite good at using the POPS process to facilitate 'all-win' agreements among employees. It looks like that's what he might be up to right now."

Tom could see that the manager was having a meeting with two people. "Let's wait a few minutes and see if the meeting is winding down," Carl said.

Tom noticed that Sam, a balding man with glasses, was listening carefully as the two other people talked. Occasionally, he would say something and then refer to one of two wall charts behind his desk.

Tom recognized one of the charts as the company's list of values. The other was a worksheet-type chart labeled POPS—*People-Oriented Problem Solving*.

Within five minutes, the meeting broke up and the two employees left Sam's office. They appeared satisfied with the outcome.

Sam came forward and Carl introduced him to Tom. "Hi," said Sam. "If you're with Carl, you must be learning about Managing By Values. Is there any way I could help?"

"Yes," said Tom. "Carl tells me that you have become an expert at using the POPS process to facilitate 'all-win' agreements among employees."

"I'm not sure I'm an expert, but that's what I was doing with those two folks who were in my office."

"How did it go?" wondered Tom.

"Quite well," said Sam. "I basically let the two of them work out their problem by themselves, stepping in occasionally when one person was reacting, to get him to listen and the speaker to clarify further. My role was to remind them of our guiding values and then to follow the POPS decision-making process."

"Tell me more about POPS."

"It consists of a series of questions or steps that people go through together. They are designed to lead to an action plan that will ensure that this gap situation won't occur again."

Sam pointed to the chart behind his desk. "The questions are in three phases—*Definition, Search for Solutions,* and *Implementation/Follow-Up.*"

Tom saw that there were a number of questions under each phase. As he scanned the chart, Sam highlighted each category by reading aloud some representative questions.

# POPS PROCESS©

## PHASE I:
## DEFINITION

1. CLARIFY CONCERNS
   • What are our key concerns?

2. ESTABLISH GOAL STATEMENT
   • What has to be accomplished?

3. IDENTIFY KEY REQUIREMENTS
   • Who are the key stakeholders affected?
   • What are your/their/the organization's expectations?

## PHASE II:
## SEARCH FOR SOLUTIONS

4. DETERMINE SOLUTION(S)
   • What win-win solutions can we think of?

5. EVALUATE SOLUTION(S)
   • What is/are the best solution(s) to achieve our goal?

6. OBTAIN AGREEMENT
   • What are we willing to try?

## PHASE III:
## IMPLEMENTATION/FOLLOW-UP

7. DEVELOP ACTION PLAN
   • What has to be done to make this solution work?

8. ESTABLISH MEASUREMENT PLAN
   • How will we know if the plan is working?

9. FOLLOW-UP RESULTS
   • How well did this solution work?
   • What could we have done differently to get better results?

"Could you give me an example of how it's used?" asked Tom.

"Sure," smiled Sam. "In our company, one of the primary values is being Ethical. When it comes to our employees, one way we define this is in terms of self-esteem. You know about the research linking people's self-esteem with their performance?"

"No. But I'm learning."

"Well, there's little doubt that people who feel good about the way they are treated at work do better work. We want to 'walk' our being-Ethical talk by making sure our managers and supervisors don't damage people's self-esteem. If people perform well, we want to *enhance* their self-esteem by recognizing them. If they make a mistake, we want to correct them, but in a way that *maintains* their self-esteem. We have a saying around here that we hope keeps people out of trouble: 'Focus on the behavior, not the personality.'"

"So, let's say," Tom intervened, "that you and I work together. We get into a conflict, and I feel attacked by you." He paused, looking for help. "How could I deal with that within the POPS process?"

Sam leaned forward and said, "All you would have to do is say, 'Sam, I think we have an Ethical gap here. The way you're treating me is unethical according to how the company defines ethical behavior.'"

"And suppose you said, 'I don't think so. I'm just doing my job of keeping you on track.' What then?" wondered Tom.

"Then we'd be required to go through the POPS process together," said Sam. "We might need some help, but we'd begin by determining whether this is a situation that qualifies for POPS. We'd have to agree on whether our issue is going to slow down or halt our individual work or our working together on a project or task. We would use the POPS questions to guide us."

Tom looked doubtful. "All this sounds good, but aren't there times when people are concerned about possible negative consequences of confronting an issue—particularly if it involves the person they report to or a coworker who is hard to deal with in a conflict situation?"

"Sure," Sam replied. "When that happens, the person can request that an ombudsperson like Carl or myself sit in and facilitate the steps. We've had many opportunities to help people work through interpersonal conflicts, haven't we, Carl?"

"Sure have," said Carl. "We start by having the parties involved share their concerns about the situation, and we end with an agreement between them about how they will interact in the future in a way that is consistent with our company values. The process can take anywhere from ten minutes to several hours."

"Does every gap situation require the POPS process?" asked Tom.

"No," said Sam. "When the problem, whether a people or a task issue, is what I call 'above the surface'—that is, we don't have to deal with or process a lot of personal or interpersonal stuff—we use a *Gap Alignment Action Plan*, or GAAP. Here's a copy of a plan that we used to solve a costly problem for our company. It involved a lack of common understanding and cooperation between the Sales and Collections Departments."

## Gap Alignment Action Plan©

| | |
|---|---|
| **Step 1:** | **The Value/Standard Principle = Ethical** (*doing right by all key stakeholders*) |
| **Step 2:**<br>*Current* State:<br><br><br>*Desired* State: | **The Gap**<br>Many requests from Sales not to push for collections and requests to "go easy" on customer collections<br>Credit and Collections believe that our company's success value requires us to treat others *fairly* but *firmly* |
| **Step 3:**<br><br><br><br><br><br><br>Success Indicator:<br><br><br><br>Success Indicator: | **"Desired State" Performance Indicators**<br>*(Note: The degree of achieved results can be measured at differing levels of progress. Three basic levels are used here: (a) minimally acceptable results, (b) satisfactory results, and (c) outstanding results/progress at this time.)*<br>1a: Reduce 90 days past due to 10% uncollected<br>1b: Reduce 90 days past due to 5% uncollected<br>1c: Reduce 60 days past due to less than 5% uncollected<br>2a: Meet with all Sales personnel to get their understanding and commitment to company's expectations<br>2b: Sales demonstrates genuine assistance in reduction of uncollected revenues<br>2c: Support from Sales results in reduction of uncollected revenues to the satisfactory targeted level |
| **Step 4:** | **Gap Reduction Actions**<br>1. Discuss shared collection responsibilities with Sales<br>2. Explain Collections' approach to overdue accounts<br>3. Enlist support from Sales personnel in the ongoing collections process based on their customer knowledge and relationships |
| **Step 5:** | **Derived Benefit (or consequences for nonattainment)**<br>1. Personal: acceptance and support from Sales; collaboration between Sales and Collections co-workers<br>2. Organizational: provide company with financial resources, which it needs and is entitled to receive in return for its products/services |

Tom noticed that the process asked people to first
identify the value, then describe the gap that exists.
The rest of the plan seemed to involve setting a goal to
close the gap and designing action steps to get there.

"These tools, POPS and GAAP, encourage people
to be accountable," Sam said. "They force us to step
up to the plate and live our values. We can't just
sweep our feelings under the rug, like they do in many
organizations."

Tom and Carl thanked Sam for sharing his
experience and continued on their journey.

As they walked away, Tom voiced a concern.
"POPS sure seems to hold your feet to the fire with
interpersonal issues. But wasn't this process tough for
some people when you initiated it?"

Carl smiled. "Lots of people found it rough going
at one time or another. In the beginning, many people
were uncomfortable dealing with their feelings. But
gradually most of them came around. Some people
have told me heartwarming stories about how they
have used the POPS tool at home with their families.
Here's our cafeteria. How about a snack?"

After they got coffee and something to eat, the
two sat down. Tom asked, "What about the problems
that are *not* people problems? What do you use then?"

"Then we use the GAAP or TOPS tool kit. TOPS
stands for a process called *Task-Oriented Problem
Solving*. It involves a series of tools we use instead of
the GAAP when a more complicated problem exists

regarding our strategies, systems, processes, or work practices. Many of these are similar to those used in organizations that have adopted initiatives such as Total Quality Management, Work Redesign, or Process Reengineering."

"Can you give me an example of TOPS in action?" asked Tom.

"One example of a situation where we used TOPS tools was a long-standing conflict at the end of every month among our sales, accounting, and shipping departments. When we launched MBV, somebody identified this situation as a key values gap."

"What did you find out?"

"The cause of the problem was a compensation policy stating that a sale couldn't be credited to a sales month unless the product had been shipped and billed during that month. Our sales people get bonuses every month based on performance, so they wanted to get every last sale out the door."

"And that put pressure on your shipping and accounting people."

"Exactly. They were working twelve-hour days the last few days of the month. But when everybody put the issues and their perspectives on the table and began to work on solutions, it became quite easy to eliminate the pressure caused by this policy.

"Representatives from shipping, accounting, and sales worked together to come up with a whole new solution for dealing with the end-of-the-month workload crunch. Not only has it relieved the stress, it's resulted in those three departments working like one team."

"To me, that outcome in itself would be worth implementing Managing By Values!" exclaimed Tom. "We have very similar interdepartmental problems in my own company. What strikes me is the way you seem to be dealing with MBV issues almost every day."

Carl got up from where they were sitting and motioned for Tom to follow him. As they began to walk together, Carl said, "I've been reading lately the comments of leaders of organizations who have been doing reengineering. They say that compared to dealing with people's resistance to change, the streamlining of company systems is relatively easy. MBV is an answer to the resistance problem, as it gets people aligned by working on specific personal issues."

"How does that happen?" wondered Tom.

"Every person—including you, the company president—will have stated development goals," said Carl. "The goals focus on specific, key values-focused performance areas targeted to improve individual behavior, work group or team contributions, and organizational results. We call this our Performance Management Process or PMP for short."

Carl handed Tom a booklet he'd been carrying. "Here's a copy of the manual for guiding people in its proper use, consistent with MBV."

Tom leafed through the twenty-page manual and stopped at a chart in the center of it:

---

### ALIGNING PERSONAL GOALS WITH COMPANY VALUES

• What is a personal goal of mine that will fulfill the organizational goal of BEING ETHICAL?

GOAL: To _____

_____

• What is a personal goal of mine that will fulfill the organizational goal of BEING SUCCESSFUL?

GOAL: To _____

_____

• What is a personal goal of mine that will fulfill the organizational goal of BEING EXCELLENT?

GOAL: To _____

_____

---

"I'm beginning to see why people say that alignment is 80 percent of the work! People must require a lot of learning to be able to pull this off."

Carl nodded. "We've been at this for more than three years now. It all goes back to the commitment of top management, because it takes a company that long to catch on to the process and really get going with it. Now that we're on our way you'd think we could relax, but it's not true. The process of gap analysis and reduction gets clearer but not necessarily easier."

As Tom pondered this, he spied a wall plaque they were passing. He smiled and pointed to it. "Guess this is what you mean." It said:

Walking
our talk
is an
ongoing
journey.

Tom shook Carl's hand. "Thanks for the reality check. I don't think I'm going away with any pie-in-the-sky notions about this process. In fact, this has been a sobering visit. I think I'll stop and say good-bye to Alexa."

When Tom got to the president's office, Alexa greeted him with a big smile, "Well, are you squared away about the alignment phase of MBV?"

Tom nodded. "I can see why without the aligning piece all this MBV stuff would be nothing but theory.

Carl told me about that management assessment process you went through. He said the feedback required you and your senior managers to take a hard look at your own personal and team values, work styles, and adaptability. I think my situation's similar. I have to change the way I treat people. The Self First principle at work again. How did you do it?"

"Jack Cunningham made it easy," Alexa said. "He sat down with each of us to review our feedback. My management team said I tended to sort information and experiences by self rather than by others. That means that if somebody said to me, 'I'm concerned about such-and-such an issue,' I'd immediately respond with, 'You know, I am too'—and then I'd proceed to talk at length about my own perspectives."

Tom smiled as he recognized that Alexa was describing one of his own behaviors. "So you had the habit of taking the ball away from people, too."

Alexa nodded. "Effective listeners stay with their speakers. They start by gathering ideas and data from them. They keep the ball in their court. They might say, 'Tell me more' or 'How come?' Maybe this seems rudimentary, but I was so entrenched in my ways, I had to learn this stuff from the beginning—like a baby learning to walk. As soon as Jack helped me identify the behaviors I had to improve, I consciously started to work at them every day in my interactions with people. Now my team says I'm more effective as a coach and facilitator when the situation calls for it.

That helps everyone focus on Excellence—an important value for us."

Tom asked, "How about your other managers? Did everyone in your management team set their own goals to become more effective as you did?"

"Yes, they did," Alexa replied. "Every one of us had to take alignment actions based on this feedback. Many of them openly shared their goals with others who could support them. The most impressive of these was one of our key people who got feedback that others viewed her as power hungry. She'd get into controversial battles with people without even realizing it, and then they found it hard to trust her. If nothing was at stake, she was fun to work with, but the minute the stakes went up, she'd change. People didn't know who would show up on any given day—Ms. Amiable or Attila the Hun."

"Has she changed?"

Alexa nodded. "It wasn't easy for her, as you might imagine, but as soon as she had her meeting with Jack to identify her new target behaviors, she started right in. One of the best things she did was to ask people to tell her when her power plays were kicking in so she could recognize how this pattern worked—what touched it off, what feelings she could look for, and so on. I'm really proud of her. When a person like this changes, she inspires others. Her story is like many others that I keep in this book."

Alexa held up a large, impressive, leather-bound binder. The title in gold embossed lettering read *Our Journey of Values*.

"I collect Success Stories in here," Alexa continued. "It's full of pictures, memos, letters, copies of awards, and articles from our company newsletters and elsewhere. The set of letters and memos here about the manager I mentioned documents her own progressive journey from complaints to appreciation, to the praise and admiration that led others to recommit to their own self-initiative."

"It's a book of your company's living history!"

"I keep it handy as a source of inspiration for myself and others. It's actually the second one I've started, and it's already getting full, too. You'll see. As soon as you start your journey, there will be plenty of exciting stories worth documenting."

Alexa came around the desk and shook Tom's hand. "I wish you a fortunate journey, as we like to say. If I can ever be of further help, just let me know."

# VIII

# Beginning the MBV Journey

LATE THAT EVENING, Tom lingered over the notes he had taken during his visits with Telecom and Meredith Manufacturing. He thought about how well he'd been treated by the people at various levels in those organizations. They were colleagues of his now, companions on a common journey.

Recalling Jack Cunningham's Three Acts of Life, Tom realized that his new friends were strong reminders of his need to embrace Act Two, Connect. He didn't want to turn his back on the need to achieve, but he had it in a new perspective now. Despite the many unknowns that lay ahead, he felt a deep confidence about where this new road could lead both him and his company.

Early the next morning, Tom walked into a restaurant for a breakfast meeting with Jack Cunningham. Despite the fact he'd had little sleep, he was excited about starting on his company's own Fortunate 500 journey. Tom spotted Jack in a corner booth and hurried over to him. Jack's quick smile and firm handshake communicated a genuine upbeat energy that was contagious. A waitress came by and they ordered from the menu. Then they got down to business. Tom filled his companion in on the results of his two recent visits.

"I hope," said Jack, "that the people you visited made it clear that we're probably talking about at least three years before your organization is really on track with a Managing By Values culture."

Tom nodded. "I certainly understand now that MBV is not a quick fix! So where do we start?"

"I recommend that for the next few months we focus on developing clarity about your company's vision, mission, and values. This includes getting buy-in on these values from all your key stakeholders. During this initial three-month period, we'll also conduct two baseline values-based assessments—one for top management and another for the organization." Tom agreed.

"After that," Jack continued, "we'll deploy our communication initiative prior to launching into the most time-consuming phase."

"The alignment phase, right?"

"Right. I can meet with you next Friday. You and I can spend the morning together, and then I can meet with your management team in the afternoon."

"That," said Tom, "will be an important meeting. I'm not sure it will be easy getting their acceptance of our Managing By Values plan. As I told you in the beginning, my management style has been part of the problem. As a result, I doubt you'll find my team ready to jump on-board with my newest idea."

"The fact that you're so aware of this situation is a plus," replied Jack. "The reality is, it's never easy to get true commitment. In talking about sharing values, you're dealing with something that touches people deeply. What I've found is that people tend to divide into three types." Tom opened his notebook and began writing as Jack laid out the three types.

"First, you have the immediate *enthusiasts*. They love change and are ready to go along with Managing By Values as soon as they recognize its benefits to the organization. Second, there are the *blockers*. Their first reaction is to resist change, to dig in their heels. Finally, you have the *fence-sitters*. These are the 'wait-and-see' people. They want to watch what happens, see which way the wind is blowing before they decide to join the parade. This is often the largest or at least the 'swing' group."

Tom smiled. "I can imagine you'll find all three types on my team when you meet with them Friday. I can also foresee that a large segment of RimCo people will be fence-sitters." He sighed. "I'm sure glad I've got you in my corner, Jack. To be honest with you, I guess I'm feeling pretty alone at this point."

The waitress brought their breakfasts, and the two men ate in silence for some time. Then Jack said, "You might be biting off a lot here, taking on the whole company at once. Maybe you'd like to institute MBV a little more slowly, like starting with one department." Jack paused, noting how Tom's eyes lit up at his suggestion. "Do you have a unit at RimCo that has some immediate enthusiasts in it where it might be feasible to implement the MBV process?"

"I think our Marketing Department would be perfect for that. They're forward thinkers. Plus, I've got friends over there and have gotten along relatively well with everybody. How would it work?"

Jack explained, "Let me describe an activity I call *Values Negotiation and Consensus*. I've used it successfully in many different situations—from large companies, to departments within companies, to small mom-and-pop-type establishments. The purpose of the activity is to help all the people in a team or subgroup gain alignment around a set of shared values. Sometimes the exercise takes a few hours. With larger groups, a day or more might even be required. But when it's over, people feel good. They've come together around some important ideas and produced a product—a set of values they can all commit to and use to guide the way they operate together."

Tom felt a surge of hope. "Why don't you use this activity with my management team Friday? If it goes well, you could start with the Marketing Department the following week. Or, if it isn't too difficult to facilitate, maybe each manager could run it with his or her department afterward. What do you think?"

Jack laughed. He could see that Tom was getting excited again. "First, let me describe how the Values Negotiation and Consensus activity works, okay? Then we can take it from there." He sorted through his briefcase and pulled out a printed sheet of paper. Handing it to Tom, he said, "Take a look at this."

# OUR VALUES

*The most important thing in life is
to decide what is most important.*

What should our organization, department, unit, or team
stand for? What should be the values by which we operate?
Look over the list of values below. Circle any values that "jump
out" because of their importance to you. Then write your *top
three* values, in order of importance, below the list. Feel free to
add values if needed.

| | | |
|---|---|---|
| truth | persistence | resources |
| efficiency | sincerity | dependability |
| initiative | fun | trust |
| environmentalism | relationships | excellence |
| power | wisdom | teamwork |
| control | flexibility | service |
| courage | perspective | profitability |
| competition | commitment | freedom |
| excitement | recognition | friendship |
| creativity | learning | influence |
| happiness | honesty | justice |
| honor | originality | quality |
| innovation | candor | hard work |
| obedience | prosperity | responsiveness |
| financial growth | respect | fulfillment |
| community support | fairness | purposefulness |
| integrity | order | strength |
| peace | spirituality | self-control |
| loyalty | adventure | cleverness |
| clarity | cooperation | success |
| security | humor | stewardship |
| love | collaboration | support |

1. _____

2. _____

3. _____

Tom took time to look over the sheet, then nodded to show he understood it. Jack continued, "The activity works best with groups of somewhere between six and thirty participants. It begins by having each participant complete this sheet on his or her own. After everybody has chosen three values and ranked them, the fun begins. I ask people to pair up around the room and sit facing each other. Then I say, 'You and your partner have six values there between you. Your task for the next ten minutes is to share your lists, agree on *three* values from your combined list of six, and rank them in order of importance.'"

Tom found himself imagining the scene of pairs of people all around a room talking excitedly. "Can they do it?" he asked.

"Always," Jack answered. "Before they start, I remind them that a lot of the words on the list have similar meanings, and I coach them to listen carefully and see where they already agree. Also, I tell them it seems reasonable that each person should have the essence of his or her top value represented in the final three."

"What happens after pairs of people come up with three shared values? Do pairs take on pairs?"

"That's exactly right," said Jack. "Two teams of two negotiate to three values. I take time to coach them through the same process—sharing and listening and finding agreement. I give the groups twenty minutes to arrive at their lists of three values."

"Since the pattern is to double the number of participants each time, I'd guess that the next step is to go to groups of eight?" Tom said.

"Right again. The larger the groups, the longer it takes. As the groups get above four, I have them appoint spokespeople to represent them, and the rest sit around and watch. Thirty-two people would require a whole morning. You have to juggle odd numbers to include everyone. But in the end—and I've never seen it fail—you have the whole roomful of people looking at three values on a wall, and everyone is saying, 'Those are ours—all of ours.'"

Tom smiled, imagining that outcome for his management team. "That sounds great," he said. "So that's the Values Negotiation and Consensus activity?"

"Only the first phase of it," Jack replied. "In the afternoon of that day, or at a later date, the same people come back and divide themselves into three equal-sized groups to work on what I call 'behaviorizing' the values. Each group takes a value and begins to define what that value would look like in operation—all the ways they can think of, given their corporate culture, that the value might be acted out. Then each group presents its list to the others. At the end of the session, people are feeling like they've really done valuable work. They've come up with a set of shared operating values, and they've thought about how to make those values impact the way they work together.

"I praise their efforts, and then I say, 'Now, the only way this will have any payoff in terms of the actual way you operate together is to agree that these three values are now the *boss*. That is, any team decision or conflict or difference of opinion must be resolved or governed by its alignment with these values.' For instance, if the top value is Respect, then whenever somebody feels ill treated, he or she needs to holler out to those involved that this is a breach of the Respect value."

"It sounds like a mini-version of the POPS process I heard about," Tom said.

"In many ways," replied Jack, smiling. "Looks like you've done your homework on the Managing By Values tool kit."

Before they ended their meeting, Tom and Jack agreed to have Jack run the Values Negotiation and Consensus exercise with RimCo's management team that Friday. Depending on how it went, they would plan the next steps.

\* \* \*

The next few weeks were turning points at RimCo, although only certain people realized it. Jack Cunningham had instructed Tom to inform the team ahead of time about the meeting with Jack and its purpose. At the meeting, Tom briefly introduced Jack to the team and then left the room.

Jack had secured Tom's permission to share his own perceptions with the executive management team about their boss and his new direction, so he started off by telling the managers about his meetings with Tom and of Tom's visits to the other sites. "As you know," he said, "Tom is excited about Managing By Values. One of his concerns is that his own way of managing is responsible for some of the trouble this company is in, and he feels that MBV will help him to change his behavior too. I guess you all have experienced Tom's management style." The group nodded and murmured grimly.

The managers started to share their views, concerns, and aspirations. At first it was more of a venting session. As Tom had thought, his team expressed feelings of frustration, pain, and anger about the way it had been treated, but even stronger feelings about the way Tom's management style had hurt morale and productivity. As Jack listened, he began to sense that there was a genuine shared commitment to effectiveness and success. This realization, and his expertise in showing he understood what each person was saying, finally won the group over. The managers understood that he had not been hired to sell them on something or push them around.

Jack then asked the group's permission to explain briefly how the Managing By Values process worked. He covered the three phases quickly. Then he told the team members he wanted to involve them in a

structured activity that would help them consider a
possible set of values to guide the company. The group
agreed, and he began the Values Negotiation and
Consensus activity he had described to Tom the
previous week. By the end of that day, the
management team began to buy into the MBV
process. The managers were excited about the three
values they'd chosen—*Integrity, Success,* and *Service.*
The managers had worked to define the values in
terms of operating behavior. During the afternoon
break, Jack was approached by the head of finance,
Jerry Santana, who smiled and said, "I've been at
RimCo fifteen years, and this is just about the first
time we've ever agreed on anything!"

The managers were so taken by this brief
experience of MBV that they wanted to help Tom
implement it in the company. A series of meetings
were held at which Jack and Tom explained MBV
further. It was decided that the Marketing and
Finance Departments would initially pilot the process.
The managers of these departments would run their
people through the Values Negotiation and Consensus
activity and feedback focus groups during the next
month. The rest of the year, these two departments
and the executive team would attempt to manage by
their prescribed values.

The success stories from the pilot work the first
year laid the groundwork to begin MBV companywide
the next year. The first task was to finalize the

company's values. With the groundwork already done, this task did not take as long as usual.

As the company moved into the communicating phase, posters, plaques, wallet-sized job aids, and other reminders were produced and continually made visible for awareness and to encourage the use of company values in common daily situations. Articles and success stories began to appear regularly in the company newsletter, which was renamed and refocused to reflect the company's values and desired image. Soon, routine meetings were characterized by talk and actions that incorporated these values. It was hard for even the most casual visitor to RimCo to ignore its values message of Integrity, Success, and Service.

As the organization moved into the real work, the Aligning Phase, Tom was amazed at the number of gaps that were continually uncovered. He began to see that once a leader has his people's attention and their buy-in on a set of values, they are more and more willing to speak out about and act on those values.

One day as he was talking to Jack in his office, Tom exclaimed, "This MBV process has turned out to be like switching on a light bulb. I'm embarrassed to say that important gaps are coming to light in every corner of the company—and I never even knew they were there!" Jack just smiled.

Tom fished out two framed slogans from behind a filing cabinet and showed them to Jack. He explained

that they had hung in the lobby long before the MBV
initiative. One read "Customer service is not just the
Customer Service Department's job—it's everyone's!"
The other plaque solemnly intoned "Our people are
our most important resource."

"See this baloney?" smiled Tom. "I never would
have called it that before, but the input and actions
that are now being addressed in our gap reduction
efforts have proven that those statements were
nothing but empty words in terms of our practices
before MBV was instituted.

"Take this first one," Tom said, holding up the
customer service slogan. "Do you know how hard it is
to fulfill this message about customer service being
everyone's job in an organization this size? Many
people don't get it without awareness communications,
a lot of training, and follow-up coaching.

"Some department managers are reporting that
our efforts in this area these past months are
beginning to pay off—their people are starting to
relate what they do to serve our customers. But the
other aspect is perhaps almost as critical—our
relationships with each other as internal customers.
Until people at RimCo realize that they're serving one
another through their jobs, we don't have much hope
of reaching our goal of being number one in our
industry."

"What about the other slogan: 'People are our
most important resource'?" Jack asked.

"My managers would agree that people should be treated fairly and with respect—they would have agreed before. But it's hard to break old practices. Managers often take only a reactive view of this."

"As opposed to a proactive view," Jack put in.

"Right. In the reactive view, a saying like this is seen by managers as a warning not to court trouble by being too rough on employees. It amounts to, 'Get people to carry out your orders and decisions—but be nice to them.' In the proactive view, managers start acting like their people bring their brains and hearts to work—they share the power of decision making, ask people for their opinions, let them carry the ball."

"So how's it going on that front?"

Tom rolled his eyes to the ceiling and sighed. "As I said earlier, old habits die hard. We asked managers to let go of being judges, critics, and evaluators and to start being coaches, supporters, and facilitators. We redefined the role of managers and supervisors by asking them to change from a command-and-control approach to one of developing people and teams. This meant we needed to provide people with training and coaching in these management practices. We also had to make sure our performance management and recognition systems supported this new role. Sometimes it felt like we were taking two steps forward and one step back."

"Tom," said Jack with some concern, "you're one of the most enthusiastic backers of MBV I've ever seen out of the gate. But I suggest you temper your enthusiasm with patience. Remember, you can't realistically expect consistent and major results from the organization as a whole until around the third year. Progress yes, but consistent results take more time and concerted effort."

"I do know that," Tom replied sheepishly. "That's why my own personal improvement program is so important. I don't want to end up being accused again of managing by fear. I want to build and support genuine consensus based on our shared values!"

"How are you coming along on that score?"

Tom was about to answer, then smiled and sat back in his chair. "Jack," he said, "I'm glad you asked that question. But before I answer, let me make sure I know what you're really asking me. It sounds like you'd really like to know about my progress with my listening skills. Is that right?"

"Nice progress," Jack responded with an encouraging smile.

## IX

# Reflecting Back on the Journey

TOM YEOMANS SAT at his desk at RimCo, idly working the lever on his Alignment Puzzle. He could scarcely believe that three years had passed since Jack had given it to him.

The first year of RimCo's MBV journey, Tom had focused on himself, the management team, and the two pilot departments. At the end of that experimental year, enough other people in the company had come aboard that an official companywide kickoff event was launched. Since then, many people had come to regard that initial kickoff of MBV as the beginning of a reborn RimCo.

Tonight was the third annual "New RimCo" rally. Since the first spectacular event, this celebration had become a popular new tradition. It involved celebrating the MBV success stories from the year before and setting the plans for the MBV focus for the following year.

There was a knock at the door. Tom hastened to open it, as he sensed it might be Jack Cunningham. Jack was there to help finalize the plans for the MBV rally that night.

"Well," Jack began, "tomorrow it will be three years since the day you began the MBV journey at RimCo. It's been a while since we've talked about your progress. I'm glad to be here to help you prepare for your keynote speech. So, what kind of meaningful payoffs have you seen to date from your investment? I assume that's one thing you're going to talk about."

"That's for sure. The atmosphere in the organization has shifted pretty dramatically," Tom replied. "There's no question it's a better place to work now. Everyone seems to be pulling in the same direction under our new boss."

Tom held up the Alignment Puzzle, adding, "I could almost say it's beginning to work like this little machine you gave me. The values are beginning to act like a powerful magnet, aligning us around a common theme—our shared values."

"So things have taken off?" Jack asked.

"The energy is becoming contagious. People are stimulated by one another's enthusiasm and say they have a sense of renewed hope or faith from the success stories they keep hearing about and seeing happen. The impact on people's personal lives as well as work has been one of the most exciting breakthrough aspects for me."

Jack nodded, then paused. "The change in people's personal lives is always a truly satisfying and inspiring bonus," he said. "How about your own journey?"

Tom's face brightened. "This past year I've finally begun to like what I see in the mirror. I guess some other people might even agree with me."

"Have you been getting some positive feedback in this regard?" Jack inquired.

"What I'm hearing makes me think I'm making satisfactory progress, though it's taken a lot longer than I'd expected," Tom responded in a humble tone.

"Well, I'm warning you," Jack smiled. "I'm seated next to Leslie tonight at the dinner before the celebration, so I'll have a great opportunity to check with her about this." His tone changed to a more serious one. "I'm also curious to know whether your own enjoyment level with your job has changed."

"One real difference," said Tom, "is that my life isn't compartmentalized like it used to be. It used to be work, then family, then community—they were all nice little separate worlds that I never connected. Now my life has a clear, overarching purpose to it. No matter which life arena I'm operating in, it's driven by the connections between my own personal values and our company's values. Instead of a lot of separate pieces, it's all beginning to merge into one terrific integrated pie."

"Great!" said Jack. "Working just like a magnetic attractor, right?"

"Right!" smiled Tom. "I've been trying to demonstrate personal integrity by being open and honest with others, and I've been trying to build trust by putting my commitments into action. I've asked people to tell me when I fail to do this, using one of our values-alignment tools. And they have, by calling a POPS or scheduling a GAAP session.

"Well, that's enough about me for now," continued Tom. "Let's switch the focus to our company's collective MBV success. I knew you'd also want to speak to the other managers, so I set up a meeting in the room down the hall. Let's go join them, shall we?"

When they reached the meeting room, everybody greeted Jack and Tom warmly. The good-natured kidding that went on showed that Jack was looked upon as part of the group. Everyone sat down as Tom started the meeting. "Thanks for coming. As you know, it's been three years since we began our MBV journey. We would like to hear your observations about the experience as well as your feedback on my own role in it. No holds barred—give it to us straight. You all know that's our RimCo way now."

"Let me second that," Jack chimed in. "I want to hear your insights and reactions, positive or negative, to the journey. What has Managing By Values meant to you?"

Jim Channing, the vice president of research and development, was first to speak up. "What I've learned is that *Managing By Values is not just another program—it's a way of life.* It's become a way of doing business for us, not only on the outside in dealing with customers and suppliers but also on the inside in dealing with each other.

"When we first started, I just wished MBV would go away. I thought it would get in the way of our marketing. Now I realize it's exactly *the* way we should market our business. I see MBV as our unique competitive advantage as we move forward in positioning our products and services with customers."

Jack raised a question. "What do you mean by 'our unique competitive advantage'?"

"People outside RimCo—customers, suppliers, community leaders—like doing business with a company that has a strong set of operating values like ours that are the real rules between us, not just a slick set of empty half-truths."

Next came the director of human resources development, Mo Perry. "Throughout the process, I've been taking notes and keeping track of what people have told me about their experiences and reactions. I've identified a pattern, a sequence of reactions that people report they commonly experience with the MBV Implementation Process."

Mo went over to a flip chart and listed the sequence. There were seven steps in all.

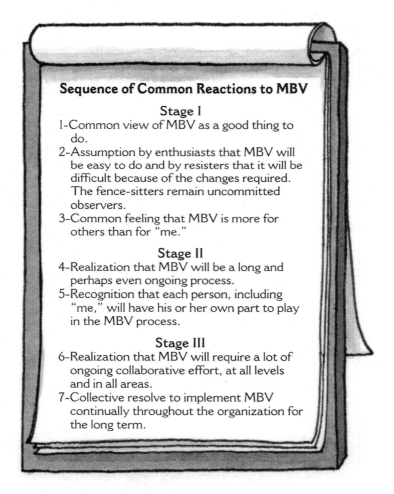

### Sequence of Common Reactions to MBV

#### Stage I

1-Common view of MBV as a good thing to do.

2-Assumption by enthusiasts that MBV will be easy to do and by resisters that it will be difficult because of the changes required. The fence-sitters remain uncommitted observers.

3-Common feeling that MBV is more for others than for "me."

#### Stage II

4-Realization that MBV will be a long and perhaps even ongoing process.

5-Recognition that each person, including "me," will have his or her own part to play in the MBV process.

#### Stage III

6-Realization that MBV will require a lot of ongoing collaborative effort, at all levels and in all areas.

7-Collective resolve to implement MBV continually throughout the organization for the long term.

"As I see it," Mo went on, "the first step on the path to implementing Managing By Values in a company like ours is genuine acceptance of its business philosophy by everybody involved. People have to believe that MBV is in the best interests of the organization and all its key stakeholder groups over time. As you know, this didn't ring true initially. In fact, it took a full year, including the experiments we did with piloting, before people began to say 'Aha, this really does make sense. It's not just a lot of fluff!'"

Jack nodded. "In other organizations where we've worked, the strongest support seemed to come from employees and frontline supervisors—even though MBV was often approached with skepticism based on their experience with other flavor-of-the-month programs that didn't work or last long. That's why it was important, Tom, for you and the executive team to first work on yourselves with the MBV process, to give it greater credibility as a change process for everyone before launching it companywide."

Mo said, "Once MBV was accepted as a sound business philosophy, some people assumed it was going to be easy to implement. They thought it was simply a new name for what we were already doing. Others felt that since upper management was behind it, Managing By Values might transform the company overnight. All we had to do was send out memos and put up wall charts and it was done. The resisters soon let these people know that this was a pipe dream."

"I remember a lot of people naively commented that this was going to be a piece of cake," Tom said. "It didn't seem to matter when I told them that wasn't the

case in the other companies I visited. They said, 'Yes,
but we're different.'"

"Everyone has to learn things for themselves,"
smiled Jim Channing. "That's why I was quick to
volunteer our department for the first year. Many took
the attitude that while we ourselves didn't need
Managing By Values, it would probably be good for
'those other people who do need it.'" People laughed
at the way Jim said this.

"So they were fully aligned with the company's
values already, and it was really all those other people
who required the help, is that it?" Jack chuckled.
Suddenly his mood became more reflective. "All these
viewpoints are understandable and to be expected.
They're typical of the way many people view any
impending changes.

"You may engineer things to look different on the
outside, but real change doesn't happen until it
happens inside people, in the way they take in and
react to situations. Since that inside change hadn't yet
occurred back when we first started, people only
changed what they saw—not what they saw *with*. It's
often not until we change what we see *with* that real
change occurs." I feel strongly that:

> When we begin to view our experiences in a different light, that's when significant breakthroughs occur in our lives.

"You know," said Tom excitedly, "you're talking about the difference I saw in those MBV project companies I visited. It wasn't that they had the best people, or more resources, or some extraordinary business strategy or plan. The difference was that the three-part process for putting Managing By Values into action really shifted people's perceptions."

Everybody sat and thought about that for a few moments. Then Caroline Swayze, vice president of finance, spoke up. "It wasn't until we were well into this process that I began to realize that Managing By Values wasn't going to be an easy thing to pull off. By that time, almost everyone was committed to the concept of MBV because of personally satisfying experiences using the POPS, TOPS, or other gap alignment tools. But they also began to recognize more situations where these tools were needed to solve the problems coming out of our corporate closets. Put that together with the realization that it wasn't going to be easy, and you have the fifth reaction noted on Mo's chart: the realization that MBV is *everybody's* business. I call it the self-ownership part of MBV."

"Are you saying that once this process has begun, there's something about it that almost seems to pull you along with it?" asked Jack.

"Yes," said Caroline. "That's when you realize that just complying with the MBV process isn't enough. The reason companywide personal growth is so key is that we have to address our own individual and group behavior to see if it aligns with our company's values. Sometimes that can be quite painful. But every time there's a showdown, we have to confront what we all said is most important—to satisfy our respective, and common, best business interests."

Paul Sherokian, head of shipping, had been quiet until now. "In order to work," he said, "Managing By Values has to be done all of the time, in all areas, with all of our stakeholder groups, and at all levels— starting at the top! When it isn't done that way, the results are predictable—it doesn't have the intended impact. We've got a saying about that in our area."

> It's easy to spot *commitment*
> when you see it—and even
> easier when you don't.

"I second that," commented Mo, adding, "These seven reactions describe a common pattern, not the only one. It isn't that everybody experienced these stages in a uniform way. But no matter what paths people took, nearly all tended to report the seventh reaction—collective resolve to continue the process.

"Today, nearly everyone in the company wants to keep going—they see the MBV process as unending. People are saying, 'We should have done this a long time ago' or 'It's hard to think of any other way to operate in the future' or 'This is why I love coming to work here every day.'"

"This is great stuff we're hearing," Jack said. "What do you say, folks?" The whole group applauded.

"I was wondering when we were going to start celebrating and acknowledging each other's successes," said Marty Driscoll, vice president of operations. "I really like the shift in our culture's focus from our previous habit of emphasizing what people were doing wrong all the time to catching each other doing things right."

"While you've got the floor, Marty," said Jack, "would you be willing to share your experience of the MBV process up to this point?"

"Okay," said Marty. "What tied it all together for me and my people was the *MBV Game Plan* we developed. It served as a map, a practical guiding framework, for keeping us on the path on our journey as well as for getting us back on track when we went astray. I could always just glance at that chart and see where we were at that moment in time."

Marty pointed to a familiar chart on the wall:

# Managing By Values® Game Plan

## Phase 1: Clarifying Mission & Values

- Owners
- Top Management
- Unit Leaders
- Employees
- Customers
- Other Key Stakeholders

## Phase 2: Communicating

- Organization & Unit Events (meetings, celebrations, etc.)
- Communications Materials (posters, brochures, action cards, etc.)
- Formal Communications Mechanisms (newsletters, etc.)
- Informal Communications Practices (memos, phone-mail messages, e-mail, etc.)

## Phase 3: Aligning Our Values with Our Daily Practices

### Individual Practices

- Self-Management & Development
- Problem Solving & Decision Making
- Leadership Practices

### Team Practices

- Effective Member Practices
- Group Dynamics & Processes
- Stages of Building High-Performing Teams
- Team/Group Facilitation

### Organizational Practices

- Strategic Management & Development
- Organizational Systems & Processes
- Resources-Barriers Management
- Rewards & Recognition Practices

### Continuous Improvement

- Review
- Reevaluation
- Ongoing Action

Everyone took a few minutes to read the MBV Game Plan. Then Marty added, "This is the fifth company I've worked for in my career and the first one where I've had the opportunity to continuously develop myself. It's an exciting place to work."

A young corporate lawyer, Jay Burningham, sought the floor. "I thought you might benefit from a legal opinion of Managing By Values. In my legal training, they taught us a lot about the law but very little about applied ethics. For me, working here in this MBV culture has been like a real-world test of my formal preparation. I've come to realize that our company's value of being Ethical captures the spirit of what justice is all about.

"Before MBV, both my education and practice of law focused on only one question: Is it legal? The three-point *Ethics Check* tool Jack taught us has broadened my inquiry. Now when I'm questioning myself about a decision I'm about to make, I ask myself; (1) Is it legal? (2) Is it balanced or fair? (3) How will it make me feel about myself? as well as, How will it make us, or others, feel about our company?

"When we add these considerations about fairness and the impact on our sense of individual and collective esteem to the legal part, we're much more likely to act in alignment with our shared Ethical value."

"It sounds," said Jack, "like you've come to recognize the true power that ethical management can have for people in managing their business."

"And their lives!" added Jay.

"Speaking of our lives," said Tom, "MBV helped me figure out not only what I wanted from my job but more importantly, what I wanted from life itself."

"How's that?" somebody asked.

"I've lived nearly fifty years without ever taking the time to think about what was important to me in life," Tom answered. "Previously I'd had no way to pull together my own personal sense of purpose and aspirations. Now I've got a personal mission statement and a set of operating values to guide my choices."

"Would you share your mission statement with us?" Jack asked.

"Sure," said Tom. "My mission is to teach myself and others how to bring out the best in ourselves so that we can better accomplish our goals and gain more satisfaction. My three prioritized personal values for fulfilling this purpose in life are integrity, love, and success."

When he finished, everyone applauded. Tom beamed and said, "The night I shared this with Leslie and the kids, I broke down. For the first time, I could explain to them my hopes and dreams about the kind of husband and father I wanted to be. I asked for their help in pointing out gaps in my behavior and helping me align myself with my own mission and values. At the same time, I began to ask each of you to help me do the same at work. With my important bases covered, I couldn't get away with any of my old dysfunctional behavior, at work or at home. It's been quite a trip, that's for sure."

"Hey," Jack commented in a tongue-in-cheek tone, "what is all this about integration of work and home? Didn't you ever hear the old saying about leaving your personal life at the door when you come to work?"

Tom smiled and said, "Yeah, that's what I did for years, when the only act in life I focused on was Achieve."

Jack said, "Now that you've heard Tom talk about the impact of MBV on his own life, would anyone like to tell Tom about *his* impact on *their* life?"

Beverly Jameson, a senior manager, waved her hand. Smiling, she said, "I think we should wait for tonight, for our celebration dinner, to do that." Heads nodded enthusiastically, and so it was agreed. The meeting ended.

As they walked down the hall, Tom said, "That was an important meeting. There's real value in periodically taking the time to look back, isn't there?"

"Absolutely," replied Jack. "It helps people to keep moving forward on the journey."

"I'm anxious to hear more about what people have to say tonight," said Tom, "not only our company's people but also the other guests—our key customers, suppliers, investors, financiers, and family members."

*   *   *

That evening Jack circulated among the festive crowd, collecting stories. Everyone seemed to be in the mood to share their experiences with Managing By Values. Jack heard comments like these:

Longtime Customer: "Dealing with RimCo since they began Managing By Values has changed our expectations and deepened our relationship. MBV is the most credible marketing tool a company could possibly have."

New Customer: "When RimCo shared its mission and values with us, we thought, 'Sure, sounds good.' Then we discovered they really mean it. This company really does walk its talk, and that's becoming increasingly hard to find nowadays. You just don't expect to get stuck with nonperforming products or service people who are rude at RimCo. They really do deliver on their promises."

Customer: "RimCo has a recovery process I wish our other suppliers would adopt. Things rarely go wrong. But if they do, we know we can speak up, be listened to with respect, and then get a satisfactory response."

Supplier: "You have to hassle most companies for payment, but not this company. They pay their bills and keep their agreements."

Financier: "RimCo is a living example of a famous saying in the banking business that neither profit and loss statements nor balance sheets determine whether an organization will pay what it owes or honor its commitments to others—it's the character of its people that determines this."

Supplier: "It's also important to realize that RimCo got the highest industry ratings for service and delivery the past two years—higher than even my own company, and we've had a consistent history of solid performance in these areas."

(Jack thought, "Imagine a supplier admitting that somebody else was better at delivery and service than they were!")

Shareholder: "Owning a piece of this company makes me proud. What goes on at RimCo has personal meaning for me. I'm pleased with the company's favorable financial gains, particularly this past year, but I really feel a sense of pride in this company—like it's *my* company."

Jack also spoke to a number of employees and their spouses. He heard many stories about changes in households as a result of the MBV process at work. One RimCo associate's husband was the town mayor. He spoke with conviction about the company's participation in civic and humanitarian projects.

Again, on a personal level, Tom's wife, Leslie, was one of the strongest cheerleaders for the MBV process. "Everyone in our family has noticed the difference," she said. "Tom's more enjoyable to live with now—and so are we!"

# X

# Moving Forward
on the Journey

THE FOLLOWING WEEK, Tom Yeomans was
sitting at his desk at RimCo, deep in thought. In a
few minutes he would be meeting with Kara Martin,
the young president of a swiftly rising cosmetics
company. Jack Cunningham had called Tom to set an
appointment with Kara as a precondition to beginning
her own company's Fortunate 500 journey.

Tom was recalling the events from the celebration
dinner the week before. In addition to a series of MBV
success story testimonials, there had been a number of
awards given to individuals and teams who had played
key roles in moving the company forward on the MBV
journey. Sitting here now, Tom replayed them all again.

At the end of the award presentations, Beverly
Jameson had gone to the microphone and stood

looking straight at him. "I know, Tom," she had said, "that I speak for the entire management team in saying that when you came back with the notion of instituting Managing By Values here, many of us were quite skeptical. We knew that some key changes could help. But frankly speaking, people felt there were problems with the way you were working with us back then, and we weren't sure about your ability to succeed in getting the company behind any new approach."

Bev continued, "Your own unwavering enthusiasm and commitment to Managing By Values, plus your willingness to learn, to grow, and to change yourself, set the stage for me and the others to sign up for this journey with you."

Tom glanced at Leslie, sitting beside him. She was beaming at him, her eyes full of pride.

"Since then, as we've been hearing tonight, there have been a lot of tremendous success stories happening to us at RimCo. But perhaps none has been the equal of the change we've seen these past two years in you." Bev paused for a moment before going on. "Tom Yeomans, you are becoming one of those rare creatures, a leader who listens and cares. You *are* now a kinder manager, a more honest co-worker, and a real partner with us all." She held up a big bronze plaque. "It's a pleasure to award one final RimCo Recognition award for Managing By Values heroism to our president and CEO, Tom Yeomans!"

Tom couldn't remember what he'd said as he received the award, but now as he gazed at it there on his office wall, he experienced a feeling of thankfulness and well-being. His thoughts shifted to the Managing By Values journey that he and his RimCo colleagues had been on together over the last three years. As his mind reviewed all the events that had occurred, his eyes caught the quotes he had put together a few days before to summarize the MBV process.

# Managing By Values Process: Key Principles

### Phase I: Gaining Clarity

- "The problem with being in a rat race is that even if you win the race, you're still a rat."
- "The most important thing in life is to decide what is most important."
- "In an organization that truly manages by its values, there is only one boss—the company's values."
- "Managing By Values is not just another program, it's a way of life."

### Phase II: Communicating Effectively

- "Genuine success does not come from proclaiming our values but from consistently putting them into daily action."
- "Communicating happens naturally when you make the work environment safe."
- "Real change doesn't happen until it happens inside people. It's a change not in what people see but in what they see with."
- "The secret to making Managing By Values work is doing what we all believe and believing in what we do."

### Phase III: Aligning Practices

- "Being values-aligned does not occur without changes in our habits, practices, and attitudes."
- "It's easy to spot commitment when you see it—and even easier when you don't."
- "Organizations don't make Managing By Values work—people do."
- "When aligned around shared values and united in a common purpose, ordinary people accomplish extraordinary results and give their organization a competitive edge."

Managing By Values had come along just in time for Tom and everyone at RimCo. Somehow it had turned out that he was one of those truly fortunate ones, who in times of change recreate their own lives and in the process, help many others do the same.

Tom winked at the award plaque as he said, "You ain't seen nothin' from *us* yet!"

# Acknowledgments

THIS BOOK IS DEDICATED to our families, friends, colleagues, "coaches," and significant others who have believed in *Managing By Values* enough to practice it within their organizations and who, in the process, have contributed to its development.

There are several people we want to thank for their support and contributions.

- *Jim Ballard* for taking our draft and further bringing the *Managing By Values* story to life with his creative writing talents. He's the best!

- *Sid Cohen, Paul Baszucki, Richard Cohen, Marcia Ballinger, Karen Clary,* and all the wonderful Norstan employees who work with them, for their pioneering spirit and visionary leadership in sticking with their Fortunate 500 journey. In so many ways, they continue to produce better results for all their stakeholder groups while also enriching people's lives.

- *Erv Kamm,* former COO at Norstan and now CEO at Digi International, for his admirable leadership, character, and unwavering commitment to the inherent principles of "ethical management," put into practice through the MBV process and tools.

- All of the good folks at the Holt Companies for their genuine belief and diligence in "walking their company's values talk"—during both the good times and the difficult times they experienced. Special recognition goes to *B. D. Holt, Peter Holt, Pete Refakis, Allyn Archer, Dave Morgan, Larry Mills,* and *Ann Cass.*

- Our many other subsequent client organizations and their true "values champions" at all levels and in all areas, for the continuing commitment to providing clarity, effective communications, and benefit-producing alignment from the wonderful contributions being sustained and created through their daily actions.

- The board members of the Fortunate Companies Foundation for volunteering their time, energy, and wisdom to advancing the Fortunate 500 business philosophy through the Managing By Values process.

- Our BTD associates for their good work and support in our initial Fortunate 500 project organizations—with special appreciation to *Greg Kaiser, Drea Zigarmi, Fred Finch, Don Carew, Reggie Tyler, Bill Eastman, Ray Snyder, Laurie Hawkins, Eunice Parisi-Carew,* and *Dale Truax.*

- And to our other colleagues serving our clients through the MBV Consultancy Group, including *Bob Patterson, Clare Paulson,* and *Marv Crowson.*

- *Harry Paul* and *Michele Jansen* for their talent and support in making our self-published version of this book become a reality through their diligent commitment to the project despite the many other balls they had to juggle.
- *Mary Falvey Fuller* for her early pioneering work and Fortunate 500 consulting contributions.
- *Wendy Seitzinger* and *Gail Strader* of the Fortunate Companies Foundation; *Amy Gourley* and *Debby Talucci* from Modern Clerical Management in Skaneateles, New York; and *Eleanor Terndrup* of Blanchard Training and Development, Inc., for their helpful and skilled secretarial support in the preparation of this manuscript.
- *Bob Nelson* at Blanchard Training and Development, Inc., for his editorial suggestions and feedback.
- *Steven Piersanti,* the president of Berrett-Koehler Publishers, Inc., for giving and securing from others helpful editorial feedback. This version reflects that constructive criticism.
- And, most importantly, *Margie Blanchard* and *Mary Ann O'Connor* for their constant love, encouragement, and continuing support for each of our lifework.

# About the Authors

KEN BLANCHARD, PH.D., is a world-renowned, best-selling author, speaker, and business consultant. His classic book, *The One Minute Manager,* coauthored with Spencer Johnson, still appears on the *New York Times* and *Business Week* best-seller lists fifteen years after its publication, along with his more recent coauthored books *Mission Possible, Raving Fans, Everyone's a Coach,* and *Empowerment Takes More Than a Minute.* The Managing By Values® process embodies his entire leadership and management philosophy. As a speaker, Blanchard has received the highest possible recognition: Toastmasters International's coveted Golden Gavel Award and the Council of Peers Award of Excellence (CPAE) from the National Speakers Association. His companies, Blanchard Training and Development, Inc., a full-service training and consulting company cofounded with his wife, Marjorie, and Blanchard Solutions, have worked with many of the leading Fortune 500 companies and fast-growing entrepreneurial enterprises. The Blanchards live in San Diego.

MICHAEL O'CONNOR, PH.D., is founder of the Center for Managing By Values and creator of the MBV process, a culmination of over twenty-five years of research. He is called upon daily to provide his expertise in the areas of personal, group, and organizational behavior. His role often can be described as Executive Coach, "master consultant to consultants" or "master trainer of trainers." His coauthored books include *The Platinum Rule, People Smart,* and *Mysteries of Motivation.* O'Connor has three decades of experience conducting conferences and seminars, developing programs and learning materials, and consulting worldwide in the fields of leadership, conflict resolution, behavioral management, values development, and organizational change. Besides his work as Director of Consultancy Services for the Center for Managing By Values, O'Connor is also Founder and Chairman of the Board of the Life Group of Companies—a group of family-owned businesses. He resides with his wife, Mary Ann, in Naples, Florida.

# Services Available

IMPLEMENTATION of the Managing By Values process is a joint venture between the Center for Managing By Values and Blanchard Training and Development, Inc.

## CENTER FOR MANAGING BY VALUES

Dr. O'Connor is director of the Center for Managing By Values. Its portfolio of services is designed for clients who aspire to learn and effectively implement "Fortunate 500" business principles and practices in their personal and organizational lives.

These services include
1. Values-based organizational development projects
2. Fortunate 500 Foundation consultancy services
3. "Champions" development programs
4. Special values-focused events
5. Values-based learning materials

For further information on Managing By Values or on Dr. O'Connor's programs and services, contact

Life Associates and the Center for Managing
By Values
122 Noxon Road
Poughkeepsie, New York 12603
Phone: (845) 454-2611
Email: customerservice@lifeassociatesinc.com

## BLANCHARD TRAINING AND DEVELOPMENT, INC.

Blanchard Training and Development, Inc. (BTD), is a
full-service management training and consulting
company located in Escondido, California. It was
cofounded in 1979 by Drs. Kenneth and Marjorie
Blanchard. BTD is in the "solutions business" and has
as its motto: "We guarantee your survival and
continual growth by helping you improve your present
operation while simultaneously creating your future
enterprise."

For further information on Managing By Values
or Dr. Blanchard's activities and programs, contact

Blanchard Training and Development, Inc.
125 State Place
Escondido, California 92029
(760) 489-5005 or (800) 728-6000 ext. 5261
Fax: (760) 489-8407

# Berrett–Koehler
## Publishers

**Berrett-Koehler** is an independent publisher dedicated to an ambitious mission: *Creating a World That Works for All*.

We believe that to truly create a better world, action is needed at all levels—individual, organizational, and societal. At the individual level, our publications help people align their lives with their values and with their aspirations for a better world. At the organizational level, our publications promote progressive leadership and management practices, socially responsible approaches to business, and humane and effective organizations. At the societal level, our publications advance social and economic justice, shared prosperity, sustainability, and new solutions to national and global issues.

A major theme of our publications is "Opening Up New Space." Berrett-Koehler titles challenge conventional thinking, introduce new ideas, and foster positive change. Their common quest is changing the underlying beliefs, mindsets, institutions, and structures that keep generating the same cycles of problems, no matter who our leaders are or what improvement programs we adopt.

We strive to practice what we preach—to operate our publishing company in line with the ideas in our books. At the core of our approach is stewardship, which we define as a deep sense of responsibility to administer the company for the benefit of all of our "stakeholder" groups: authors, customers, employees, investors, service providers, and the communities and environment around us.

We are grateful to the thousands of readers, authors, and other friends of the company who consider themselves to be part of the "BK Community." We hope that you, too, will join us in our mission.

### A BK Business Book

This book is part of our BK Business series. BK Business titles pioneer new and progressive leadership and management practices in all types of public, private, and nonprofit organizations. They promote socially responsible approaches to business, innovative organizational change methods, and more humane and effective organizations.

# Berrett–Koehler
# Publishers

A community dedicated to creating
a world that works for all

**Visit Our Website: www.bkconnection.com**

Read book excerpts, see author videos and Internet movies, read our authors' blogs, join discussion groups, download book apps, find out about the BK Affiliate Network, browse subject-area libraries of books, get special discounts, and more!

**Subscribe to Our Free E-Newsletter, the *BK Communiqué***

Be the first to hear about new publications, special discount offers, exclusive articles, news about bestsellers, and more! Get on the list for our free e-newsletter by going to **www.bkconnection.com**.

**Get Quantity Discounts**

Berrett-Koehler books are available at quantity discounts for orders of ten or more copies. Please call us toll-free at (800) 929-2929 or email us at **bkp.orders@aidcvt.com**.

**Join the BK Community**

BKcommunity.com is a virtual meeting place where people from around the world can engage with kindred spirits to create a world that works for all. **BKcommunity.com** members may create their own profiles, blog, start and participate in forums and discussion groups, post photos and videos, answer surveys, announce and register for upcoming events, and chat with others online in real time. Please join the conversation!